Second Edition

ONE VOICE

Second Edition

ONE VOICE

Integrating Singing and Theatre Voice Techniques

Joan Melton
with Kenneth Tom

WAVELAND
PRESS, INC.
Long Grove, Illinois

For information about this book, contact:
    Waveland Press, Inc.
    4180 IL Route 83, Suite 101
    Long Grove, IL 60047-9580
    (847) 634-0081
    info@waveland.com
    www.waveland.com

The authors and publisher wish to thank those who have generously given permission to reprint borrowed material:

Figures in Chapter 2, except for Figure 2–9, are reprinted from *Dynamics of the Singing Voice, Fifth Edition* by Meribeth Bunch Dayme. Copyright © 2009. Published by Springer-Verlag Wien. Reprinted by permission of the author and publisher.

Figure 2–9 is reprinted from *Principles of Voice Production* by I. R. Titze. Copyright © 2000 by the National Center for Voice and Speech. Reprinted by permission of the author and the National Center for Voice and Speech.

10-digit ISBN 1-57766-771-9
13-digit ISBN 978-1-57766-771-1

Printed in the United States of America

7   6   5   4

to
Chris and Cheryl and Jonathan

Contents

Acknowledgments

Several years ago David Carey said to me, "What about a book?" Mhairi Armstrong followed up on that suggestion by asking me periodically, "How's the book coming?" I owe a very special thanks to these two mentors for gently encouraging me to put this information in writing. As I was searching for the right title for the book, Julia Moody said, "Why not call it *One Voice*? That's what you're saying." And so it is! Thank you, Julia, for naming the book.

Sincere thanks to my friend and colleague, Kenneth Tom, with whom I am honored to have shared this project. Thanks to our first editor, Lisa Barnett, for her patience and wisdom throughout the writing process. To Evelyn Carol Case I shall always be indebted for her cheerful reading of the manuscript and brilliant suggestions. I am very grateful to the late Dorothy Mennen for reading several chapters of the book and making valuable comments and suggestions regarding its format. Special thanks to my former students, J. R. Arnold and Ty Turner, for photography; and Annie DiMartino, Chad Granier, Josh Odor, Kim Purdy, and Janine Christl, for their willingness to demonstrate the exercises. To all my students at Cal State Fullerton, along with Susan Hallman and Sallie Mitchell, department chairs, and Barbara Arms, Gladys Kares, and Debra Noble of the dance faculty, my warmest appreciation for your insightful comments and support.

Many thanks to Brett Strader for preparing the musical examples, to Marika Becz for introducing me to Ashtanga yoga, to Annie Loui for the voice/movement connections she inspired, and to Karen Shanley who rekindled my passion for movement-based work and its relationship to vocal production.

I am especially grateful to Meribeth Bunch Dayme for her inspiration and guidance, as well as her permission to use many excellent illustrations from her classic text, *Dynamics of the Singing Voice*. Sincere appreciation, also, to Ingo Titze for his kind

ix

permission to use illustrations from *Principles of Voice Production.* I am indebted to the work of Neil Semer and to his enthusiasm for the book's perspective. Sincere thanks, also, to Kevin Robison and Gerard Reidy for urging us to undertake and complete this project.

Finally, and most especially, I am deeply grateful to Catherine Fitzmaurice, whose genius and generosity of spirit have contributed immeasurably to my work and to the training of actors and singers throughout the world.

Joan Melton

It has been a great pleasure and a great privilege to be able to collaborate with Joan Melton, whose knowledge base, practical wisdom, and joy in her work are so evident here, as in all her work. Thank you, Joan, for this wonderful opportunity. I would also like to express my deep gratitude to Ingo Titze and Kittie Verdolini, who have been my mentors and models in building bridges between the art and the science of vocal production.

Kenneth Tom

Introduction

Overview

The training of singers is often very different from the training of actors. I maintain that they should be far more similar. I believe that most singers would benefit enormously from the physicality of theatre voice training and that actors would audition with greater confidence if singing were taught as one of several uses of the voice, along with speaking, laughing, crying and the variety of other vocal sounds essential to the actor's work. Speaking and singing have common denominators and finding out what they are and making them our own requires research, study, and a genuine openness to rethinking what we *know*.

Too often actors and singers feel torn between their training in the voice studio and their training as actors. Singers are concerned with voice *quality*, and particular kinds of quality, as well as with vocal health. Actors are concerned with voice as an element of characterization and as an available tool for communicating. Although actors and singers share the vocal health concern, the last thing an actor wants to do is choreograph the voice, or predetermine its particular qualities in the same way that a singer might. Singers need to sound *good*, or even beautiful, most of the time, whereas actors can use any sound that is appropriate, and *appropriate* is not always beautiful in the bel canto sense.

Musical theatre and opera necessitate an integration of music and theatre perspectives. Actors who sing and singers who act must have both (1) a concern for voice quality and (2) an unconscious availability of the *whole* instrument—body and voice—in response to impulse and imagination. Appropriate work can facilitate that integration, even for those who sing only sixteen bars of a song or brief solos and choruses in a variety of productions.

The work of Catherine Fitzmaurice figures prominently in the overall perspective and approach to voice training in this book. Fitzmaurice Voicework®, or *Destructuring/Restructuring*, effectively integrates voice and movement, and facilitates a healthy, beneficial dialogue between theatre voice training and the training of singers for a variety of media. In addition, it can be a valuable tool for the retraining and healing of virtually any voice that has been misused or abused.

In the summer of 1998, I presented the first voice workshop with Catherine Fitzmaurice in which we focused on the integration of singing and theatre voice techniques. Since then I have incorporated voice into every possible physical activity and have encouraged singers and actors to move freely from singing to speaking and vice versa. I have also incorporated singing techniques into my theatre voice classes and have developed workshops and courses designed to bridge the gap between speaking and singing on stage. Dr. Kenneth Tom has been an integral part of these activities. As a speech-language pathologist and singer, Dr. Tom contributes unusual clarity and practical insight to the understanding of voice as a single instrument capable of many actions, and his presentations in theatre voice classes and workshops have been significant and invaluable.

Students and workshop participants often ask, "Is there a book?" or "Are these exercises written down?" Vocal technique is obviously not a subject to be learned from a book and is a very individual matter indeed. However, there are principles and exercises that can be notated and discussed, and this book is our offering in that direction.

Guidelines for Using the Book and CD

The first two chapters—1, The Foundation, and 2, Vocal Anatomy and Physiology—provide essential information on which the rest of the work is based. The remaining chapters are organized in a developmental fashion but can be used separately, and/or out of sequence, once the initial sections have been grasped thoroughly. All sections apply to both actors and singers; however, Chapter 8, Special Considerations, focuses primarily on actor training and Chapter 7, Singing and Acting, focuses on the training needed by singers who may not have had an acting course.

Although the book is divided into chapters, obviously the voice and body are not separated, so when you are working on alignment, for example, you are also working on breathing, range, resonance, and articulation. Some exercises might fit nicely into more than one chapter. You should develop a daily routine based on your needs, interests, and challenges, and then allow that routine to change with the demands of your particular career.

The CD accompanying this edition is a response to requests from teachers and students alike, and is designed to supplement the instructions in the book. Many exercises do not lend themselves to a CD format, and those that are included should be learned in conjunction with the book, especially for the photo illustrations.

When doing the exercises, remember to balance technical accuracy with playful exploration. The voice is happiest when it is allowed to *play* and when it is not always being judged and predetermined. That said, the more solid the technique, the more interesting and expansive the play! All the exercises can be modified and/or adapted to individual needs, so listen to your own body, work one on one with a voice/movement practitioner whenever possible, and always consult a physician before embarking on any new fitness program, including one for your voice!

PART I

Basic Technique

1 ■ The Foundation

Alignment

Alignment alone can give you *presence* when you enter a room, *balance* when you are dancing, and the environment for every possible *resonance* in the voice. It is the first step in voice training. The body is designed to *move*, so alignment is not about being in any one position; rather, it is about moving with ease and using the body with maximum efficiency. It is about having the whole body available for characterization, unencumbered by habitual idiosyncrasies that limit the actor's exploration of physical/ vocal possibilities.

There are many approaches to aligning the body. The Alexander Technique is a wonderful route, as is Pilates; I strongly recommend both. It is important, however, to be aware of the breathing differences in some movement work, and voice work. Breathing for speaking and singing on stage requires the *release* of the abdominal muscles on inspiration and the *use* of deep abdominals and/or pelvic floor muscles on expiration. Pilates training is excellent for strengthening the muscles of the abdomen and pelvic floor and focuses considerable attention on awareness and use of the abdominal muscles. Some contractions required for Pilates, though, may need to be modified for speaking and singing.

Hatha yoga is a marvelous discipline for actors and singers to pursue, but again, be aware that the breath work in yoga may be quite different from the efficient and desirable use of breath for speaking and singing. The more dance and movement the actor and singer can do, the better; just be very aware of the breathing differences required for different kinds of activities. For example, the noisy inhalation often demonstrated by fitness trainers is particularly inappropriate for singers and actors because it sets up unnecessary tensions and uses muscles that should be relaxed in deep and efficient breathing.

EXERCISES

When your body is aligned and you are standing, a plumb line might be dropped from your ear to your shoulder to the top of your hip, or iliac crest, to your knee to the arch of your foot. If your body is not aligned, often because of muscle misuse or lack of use, your breathing will be inhibited, lung capacity may be affected, and the sound of your voice will change. Alignment is not simply a matter of repositioning the body to match the plumb line, however. Habits have been formed and muscular use has been established. As you work on alignment, your body's habitual use may change, and your visual/aural image is likely to change as well. The following exercises can heighten your awareness of your own alignment and may be done with or without sound.

Each body has its own idiosyncrasies and needs in terms of alignment, so the exercises presented here should be supplemented by individual work with a master teacher.

Strings and a Beam

You have an imaginary string attached to the top of your head. When it pulls up gently, your head floats away from your shoulders, your eyes look straight ahead, and your ears are lined up with your shoulders. Or, if you prefer, you have strings attached behind your ears that lift your head and elongate your neck. You also have strings attached to the middle of your heels. They pull down gently to ground you and to aid the two-way stretch, or lengthening, of your spine.

Where your arms meet your torso, strings pull outward to open the chest and free your upper body. Where your legs meet your torso, strings pull outward to release any tension in the pelvic/abdominal area. So, you are widened.

Move through the room feeling first the lengthening, then the widening; then put the two together. You can feel your strings anywhere, anytime, to change your appearance, your confidence level, and your *voice*. Note that you can also change levels in space without losing your length and width.

Add a beam of light and energy high on the chest as your communication link to other human beings and the rest of your environment. Try turning off your beam and dropping your strings to see what happens to you physically and emotionally. Then turn it on again and reestablish your strings to feel the difference!

The Roll Down

Stand with your feet parallel (not turned out) and in line with your hips, knees not locked, spine long and loose. Let your jaw release downward slightly so your mouth is open. Drop your head to the front and feel the weight of your head stretch the back of your neck—any stretch in the body can deepen your breathing. Now imagine that weight is getting heavier so that it rolls your torso all the way over into a dropdown so that you are hanging from your tailbone. Allow your body to *curl* on the way down, bend your knees slightly, let your arms and head dangle, and keep your weight balanced over the arches of your feet (Figure 1–1).

Roll up slowly, visualizing the uncurling from your tailbone, one vertebra at a time, until you are upright except for your head. Slowly let your head float up, gently stretching the back of your neck as you do. Your head *comes up from the back, not from the chin* and your *chin rests parallel to the floor, not tilted upward. Do not place your shoulders.* If you have really let go, your shoulders will find their own perfect balance at the top of your torso.

Repeat this exercise several times, focusing on releasing your head; allowing your torso to curl; letting go of your arms,

Figure 1–1 The Roll Down

shoulders, and jaw; and maintaining a center of balance through-out. Your upper body should neither pitch forward nor fall back at any time.

To add sound to the movement, open your mouth slightly as if you are about to yawn; be sure that the tip of your tongue falls forward, touching your lower gum ridge, and widen your throat, as in the beginning of a yawn. On the vowel, *ah*, start with a comfortable low pitch and allow the sound to get higher as you roll down (a siren). Let the sound stop when you drop. Breathe as if your lungs are in your buttocks, then start with a high sound and allow the pitch to get lower as you roll up. Don't force or strain; just allow the movement of your body to release your voice. High sounds will occur naturally when you curl and low sounds will be easy when you uncurl.

Standing Tremor

Standing with your legs hip-width apart, turn your feet inward *slightly* and keep your knees straight. Bend and straighten your knees using a very *small* vertical action. Then let your movements get even smaller and faster until you tap into a "tremor," or something the body knows and does naturally in certain situations, as in shivering. You are no longer bending and straightening your knees; instead, your body is *tremoring* in its own way and at its own tempo. You can regulate the tempo to some extent and, of course, you can stop the movement at any time. Add voice, using vowels, hums, whatever you like, throughout your range. Have fun! This is to be enjoyed! It will loosen your body so that you are freer to move and sound with ease and grace. In addition, it will give you a physical reference for the Fitzmaurice work introduced later in the chapter.

Lift the Pelvic Floor

Now stand with your feet parallel, legs hip-width apart, and check to be sure you are neither tucking your buttocks nor arching your back. Think of squeezing your sit bones together gently and feel a spiral of energy moving up your body and out the top of your head. Lift your arms to help with the sense of openness. Or think of lifting the entire floor of your pelvis; isolate the sensation and *do not tighten your buttocks*.

Relevé, or lift onto your toes, *from your pelvis*. When you come down, be sure you do not rock back onto your heels. You should feel light and lifted, and any tendency to tilt your pelvis backward and tuck your buttocks will be clearly identified. This is your *neutral*, or balanced position.

The yoga exercises described in Chapter 4 are also excellent for alignment. They are the perfect start to a daily routine and can focus a class like nothing else.

Breathing

The way we breathe has a profound effect on the sounds we produce, and cultural ideals and musical/theatrical styles strongly affect the breathing patterns of professional singers and actors throughout the world. The techniques presented here are particularly useful for actors and singers in the Western world and specifically relate to American and British theatre.

Breathing is taught in a variety of ways so that singers and actors are often confused about what is *correct*. The major questions, or points of confusion, revolve around what to do with the body, especially in the course of inhaling and exhaling, and opposing views frequently relate directly to voice training *versus* movement. For example, dancers may be taught to *close the ribs* in front so that there is no protrusion or interruption of the physical line that contributes to balance and stability in the center of the body. In contrast, singers and actors are taught to lift the sternum, which tends to *open* the ribs in front! Perhaps the most perplexing part of the breathing dilemma is that there is more than one set of right answers! Different combinations produce different results and the combination you choose, to some extent, depends upon what you want.

The choices made throughout this book are intended to support the development and use of a wide, strong, flexible pitch range within a voice that has the capability of integrating vocal qualities, or balancing *registers*. At the same time, the breath management suggested should support the separation and/or *distortion* of qualities necessary for characterization and should be equally applicable to singing and speaking.

Certain basic actions that the body has known from birth may provide the ideal model for breath management in vocal production, and what the body knows and does habitually is often quite different from those original physical actions. In other words, what may currently *feel* natural may be habitual, but not natural. Chapter 2, which focuses on the anatomy and physiology of voice use, can serve as an invaluable reference for understanding what is actually happening in the body when we breathe and when we use breath to speak or sing. Respecting what the body knows and does well automatically is an important first step in breathing efficiently on stage. This relates particularly to inhalation, which the body does really well because of the partial vacuum created in the lungs when we expel air and need to intake more to equalize pressure inside and outside the body. Translated into practical terms, this means, we *do not need* to suck in air in a *noisy* manner. When we inhale loudly, we tend to get a *shallow* breath, set up tensions in the neck and upper chest, and cause the vocal folds to work when they should be resting! Then we may produce a breathy tone, singing or speaking, to complete the cycle of inefficient and unhealthy use of the mechanism.

EXERCISES

The first exercise here is great to use with a group or on your own. It clearly demonstrates the body's ability to inhale efficiently and unobtrusively regardless of the kinds of sounds we make. In addition, it connects physical movement with sound in a rhythmic and energizing way.

Jog and Sound

Move through the room in an easy jog, arms and legs loose like a marionette (move your arms about, overhead, etc.). Blow breath out with each step, then use your voice on each step, moving throughout your range, one sound per step (rhythmic). Be very playful, no forcing or predetermining. Just allow the body to sound as you exhale, again and again and again. Move your face! Keep the exercise going for several minutes. When you stop, take note of the fact that you have neither

Figure 1–2 The Crouch

gasped for air nor felt yourself winded for lack of breath. Your body has breathed for you in the silences between the sounds (Rodgers 2002).

Now stand in neutral and start the Roll Down. Once you are hanging over, continue to the floor and go into a Crouch, or prayer position (Figure 1–2), with your arms outstretched, your knees together or separated, and your tailbone as close to your heels as possible. Feel the breath into your back and become aware of the expansion of your ribs and the release in your buttocks. Be sure your jaw is letting go; feel free to move animal-like and to release sound at any time. Sirens, high to low, seem natural and easy in this position.

All Fours

Bring yourself up to all fours, knees in line with your hips, and let your back be flat like a table. Do some gentle staccato sounds on—huh, huh, huh—using indefinite pitches and feel the action of your abdominals. If they are letting go, you'll notice a gentle upward action for each "huh," and a release downward toward the floor in between. As with Jog and Sound, the body replenishes the air you use for the "huh" each time your belly relaxes, so you never have to suck the air in!

The Sphinx

Take yourself back into the Crouch, then stretch out on your belly and let go of any feeling of holding in that you may notice in your legs and buttocks. Bring yourself into the position of the Sphinx—forearms on the ground, shoulders down, neck long (Figure 1–3). This should be a fairly easy and comfortable position. Stretch out your tongue and the rest of your face as well, eyes wide; do several gentle staccatos using indefinite pitches. In this and other positions that arch the body, you will probably find a very low, easy sound that seems to be an extension of your usual low range. The walls of your pharynx will need to be

Figure 1–3 The Sphinx

relaxed, as opposed to squeezed, however, in order to access this sound and your tongue must not over stretch. Use "huh" or "hah" on sounds of various lengths and notice the upward action of your abdominals in relation to the sounds. It's as if you have an abdominal button, or flap, that initiates each sound. Return to the Crouch and give your back time to normalize. Always curve your body following an arch so that you protect your back.

Destructuring/Restructuring

Catherine Fitzmaurice's *Destructuring/Restructuring* approach to breath work is particularly applicable to both singing and speaking. In addition, it is infinitely practical, completely reliable, and integrates well with many other perspectives on voice and movement. *Destructuring* is about letting go of habitual breathing patterns and reconnecting consciously with the autonomic nervous system, which breathes for us when we are not thinking about *how to* breathe. Tuning into this more primitive system allows us to experience the way our bodies work naturally (e.g., what moves, which way, and when), and in *Restructuring* we consciously deepen that pattern. A distinguishing feature of the Fitzmaurice work is its use of *tremors* in certain modified yoga-based positions. The tremor has been described in a number of ways, one of which is an *energy flow*. It is similar to a shiver when we are cold, or to the body's natural tendency to shake gently when muscles are fatigued. It is not a conscious shaking, however, and taps into an action the body knows deeply and is ready to do on its own. In "Breathing Is Meaning" (Fitzmaurice 1997), Catherine discusses its use in detail and workshops in the Fitzmaurice approach are available in the U.S. and abroad.

Exercises

The following exercises are an adaptation of several Destructuring positions used in sequence. These positions will deepen your breathing. They may also tap into emotions you have held tightly in various parts of your body, so as you begin to let go, do not be alarmed if you start to laugh or cry or feel silly. Think of keeping your throat wide, rather like the beginning of a yawn, release your lower jaw and allow your tongue to fall forward in your mouth so that the tip rests just at the lower gum ridge; or work with your tongue out of your mouth, with or without the lips closed. Your voice should come right out of the breath and, therefore, start with a bit of an /h/, which will discourage any tendency toward harsh glottal attacks.

Curl and Stretch

Lie on the floor on your back, then curl yourself into a ball with your arms around your knees (Figure 1–4). Be sure to *lift your head* to your knees. Squeeze your face, especially your cheeks and eyes, and release an easy high-pitched sound with your lips closed (throat open, space between your teeth). Then stretch out,

Figure 1–4 Curl

reaching with your arms and legs; stretch your face, open your eyes and mouth, and stretch your tongue out (Figure 1–5). Keeping your throat wide, release a gentle, low-pitched sound from deep within your body on "huh." Then shake out your limbs (with or without sound), and let them fall to the floor. Enjoy the letting go!

Consciously release at your hips and shoulders by turning your legs and arms inward, then let them roll or fall outward as if from the spine. If your back arches, pull your waist down gently toward the floor, then release. Let go of the jaw so that your mouth is slightly open. Close your eyes and observe the pattern of your breathing. (Place a book or pillow under your head, if needed, just enough to *align your spine on the floor.*) Do not judge, just observe, and resist the temptation to instruct your breathing pattern into whatever you think is *proper.* Observe the path of your breath and its tempo. Allow any changes that occur naturally. *Staying* with the breathing pattern you observe, *begin to release* an almost inaudible "huh" on each

Figure 1–5 Stretch

out breath. Gradually let the "huh" become more voiced and *feel* the sound in your body. It will be a simple, fluffy sound, surrounded by air. Do not get in the way, but continue to let your body lead.

Knees to One Side

Now bring your knees to your chest and drop them over to one side (Figure 1–6). Leave your shoulders on the floor and turn your head the opposite direction from your knees so that you get a diagonal stretch. Continue to observe your breathing and notice how it changes from one position to another. Use "huh," or any other gentle sound, on each out breath and repeat on the other side.

The Pelvic Lift

Return to center, knees up, feet on the floor, and the pelvis in neutral (maintaining the slight natural curve at your waist). Feel that your neck is long and consciously release any tension in

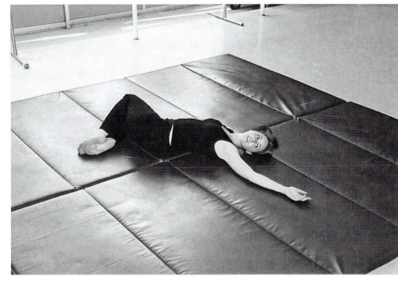

Figure 1–6 Knees to One Side

your abdominal/pelvic area. Allow your arms to be in neutral, with your shoulders released down and the palms of your hands facing the ceiling. Bring your feet fairly close to your buttocks and turn your toes inward slightly. (*Relax your toes!*) Leave your knees parallel and think of strings pulling them forward to lift your buttocks *slightly* off the ground (a pelvic tilt, or curl). *Do not* tighten the buttocks. Your lower torso and thighs relax like a hammock between your knees and your waist (Figure 1–7). A tremor, or slight shaking of the lower body, may occur naturally. The tremor will deepen your breathing, relax your body, and open up interesting resonances in your voice. Your belly should remain free. Observe your breathing and release sound, if you like, on the out breath.

Once you are used to the position and can maintain it for quite a while, your breathing and sounding may become quite irregular so that you begin to move farther away from habitual patterns. Try not to judge or censor any sounds that you think are *ugly*, or not like you. You have physical/vocal dimensions as yet

Figure 1–7 The Pelvic Lift

unrecognized and all sounds are valuable as long as they are not unsafe. Rest when you like, and hug your knees to you as you groan a deep, low-pitched sound. *Do not lift* your head this time; leave your neck long and shoulders relaxed. Rock your knees if you like.

For variation and an advanced version of the Pelvic Lift, find the position then speak gibberish to your partner on the ceiling or do a series of tongue twisters or other articulatory work using a wide variety of pitches. You may also lift your head weight with the laced fingers of your hands to access the higher pitches of your voice in an easy and playful manner.

Do not worry if a tremor does not occur in some positions or if the tremor is very slight. More is not necessarily better! Simply do the exercises, breathe, and enjoy using your voice! It may be useful to note that you will not need to work hard to get and/or maintain a tremor. Instead, you will make a slight physical adjustment, as in turning your toes inward and keeping your knees straight, at the beginning of the exercise to encourage a tremor. After that your body works on its own while you focus on resonance, range, text, intention, relationship, or whatever other aspect of your craft you choose to address.

The Dying Roach

This is a favorite exercise of many students because it is so totally involving and fun to do. Learn it in stages and modify it as necessary. (The exercise was named by Dudley Knight, Master Teacher of Fitzmaurice Voicework® and former Head of Acting at the University of California, Irvine.)

Lie on your back with your head slightly elevated, if necessary, to align your spine. Your neck should remain long and your shoulders free.

1. Lift your legs into the air at right angles to your torso. If you can maintain a neutral pelvis, keeping the slight natural curve of your spine at the waist, your belly may feel

freer. However, many people need to use a flat back or even to place pillows under the buttocks in order to find the right-angled position. Your belly should feel relatively free. Once you're there, turn your feet inward slightly and press upward gently with your heels. As with the Pelvic Lift, you will probably feel a tremor, this time in the legs. Observe your breathing and release sound if you like. Remember to let your body lead and enjoy the journey!

2. Rest your legs, then reach your arms into the air, keeping your shoulders relaxed. Let the palms of your hands face each other or turn them upward. Reach with your fingertips or with the heels of the hands, depending on your position, to get a tremor in the arms and upper body. Again, observe your breathing and release sound if you like. Then rest your arms.

3. Finally, lift both your legs and arms into the air, tremor and sound (Figure 1–8). This is the Dying Roach—or the Dying Beetle if you live in the British Isles! Rest.

Figure 1–8 The Dying Roach

Although I suggest the use of voice during most of the exercises, you may also do the work silently or with very little sound. Changing your breathing will change your voice. Throughout this book, *sound* is meant to include singing as well as non-singing, so feel free to explore as playfully as possible a whole gamut of vocal utterances and *allow* yourself to be surprised!

References

Fitzmaurice, C. 1997. "Breathing Is Meaning." *The Vocal Vision.* New York: Applause Books.

Rodgers, J. (ed.) 2002. "Jog and Sound." *The Complete Voice and Speech Workout: Book and CD.* New York: Applause Books.

2 ■ Vocal Anatomy and Physiology

Overview

Under normal circumstances, the activities of the brain, the nervous system, and the muscles involved in speech production for everyday conversation take place without much conscious effort. Until significant fatigue or serious injury occurs to any of the systems involved, we aren't usually aware of the complexity of speech production. Hundreds of highly coordinated tasks have to be accomplished every time we speak or sing: covert mental calculations, sensation messages from muscles and joints to the brain, and complex sequences of muscle activations.

In performance, demands far greater than those of everyday conversation are placed on your voice in terms of quantity, quality, and variety. You need to be audible and intelligible from a distance; vocally in character; and, hopefully, expressive—and you need to be so extensively and repeatedly. Risk for injury to the vocal cords (vocal folds) increases with such demands. A reliable and healthy vocal technique is crucial to your expressive range and longevity as a performer. Working systematically on your voice gives you access to the potential breadth of your pitch range, your loudness range, and your range of vocal qualities, as well as tools to increase the clarity of the texts you speak and sing. A fundamental working knowledge of what the body does to produce speech sounds can give you additional insights into how you are producing voice and how to reduce the risk of vocal fold injury. In this chapter, we'll take a closer look at the body structures that produce voice for speech and singing.

Physical Systems: How They Work

When people refer to the speech production mechanism, they are really using the term as a kind of shorthand for the intricately coordinated efforts of three body systems that work together: the respiratory system, the phonatory system, and the articulatory system. Before we get into more detailed descriptions of each of these systems, let's look at their *functions* in voice production.

1. The breathing system functions as a biological air *compressor*. In other words, it provides for the flow of air that is needed to produce all spoken or sung sounds. The lungs and muscles of breathing can create an incoming stream of air (like the compressor in a vacuum cleaner can), as well as an outgoing stream of air (like the compressor in a hair dryer can). The primary muscles of respiration are the diaphragm, the intercostals, and the abdominal muscles.

2. The phonatory system functions as a biological *oscillator*, which *shakes* the air stream. (*Phonation* is the production of vocal sound at the level of the larynx or voice box.) Much like the reed in the mouthpiece of a saxophone, the vocal folds vibrate, transforming an air stream into a *buzz* sound. When the vocal folds come together repeatedly during vibration, they *chop* the moving air column into little puffs of air at a regular and fast enough speed so that it creates the sound pressure waves that constitute the buzz. At this point, the vocal buzz does not have your individual sound quality, nor any speech sound characteristics. It is nonetheless the voice source, or basic material, that will later be modified into recognizable

vowels and voiced consonants. The vocal folds can also be positioned to make *frication*, or turbulence noise, which is the sound source for whispered sound and the "h" sound. After vocal buzz or turbulent noise is produced, it travels into the vocal tract above, where it is shaped into its final form.

3. The articulatory system functions as a *resonator* or *filter*. The continuous airway *tube* formed by the neighboring spaces of your pharynx, mouth, and lips is called the *vocal tract*. The sound waves of the vocal buzz made in the larynx resonate, or bounce back and forth in the vocal tract (resonance = re-sounding). This process modifies (*filters*) the sound waves of the vocal buzz into sound waves with specific phonetic characteristics (vowels and consonants) and specific vocal *timbres*—the vocal sound characteristics that make your voice recognizable as uniquely yours. In other words, the uniqueness of each speech sound you produce is a result of a specific configuration of shape and length of the vocal tract. *Articulation*, then, is the formation of sequences of vocal tract shapes that result in a series of sounds that we recognize as words. Speech articulation is primarily executed by movements of the jaw, teeth, lips, tongue, and soft palate.

Respiration

The primary job of the respiratory system is to provide oxygen to maintain life. Inhalation-related muscles around and underneath the lungs expand its size, creating a partial vacuum in the lungs, which draws in air (oxygen) from the environment. Exhalation-related muscles reduce the size of the space around the lungs, creating lung pressures high enough to expel air (carbon dioxide) from the lungs. Oxygen needs vary with the intensity of physical activity. The more intense your physical activities are, the harder the respiratory system works to increase oxygen levels (larger and more frequent breath cycles). As a secondary function, the respiratory system also provides the *excess* air stream (i.e., beyond oxygenation needs), with which we form spoken or sung phrases. The breathing mechanism is extraordinary in its capacity to draw in amounts of air greater, sometimes far greater, than needed for body oxygenation, to serve as the medium for speech. The louder you need to be, the longer the phrase you've formulated, the greater the amount of *extra* air your respiratory system needs to draw in. At low levels of physical movement, we only use about 10 to 15 percent of the lung's *vital capacity*—the amount of air that can be exhaled after a maximal inhalation; it's a bit more than a gallon of air in an average adult. During vigorous exercise, or vocalization of long and/or loud phrases in speaking or singing, it can go up to 50 percent or more.

STRUCTURAL FRAMEWORK

The skeletal framework for the respiratory system surrounds all the internal organs in the torso area and provides attachment points for muscles and soft tissue (Figure 2–1). It consists of the thorax (upper torso) and the pelvis (lower torso). The *thorax* is the part of the skeleton between the neck and the abdomen that contains the heart and the lungs (Figure 2–2). In back, it is made up of the thoracic portion of the spine (vertebral column), the shoulder blades (scapulae), and the back portions of the twelve ribs, which originate from the spine. The ribs curve around the sides of the thorax toward the front of the body, creating a barrel-like shape. In front, the upper seven ribs connect at the breastbone (*sternum*), while ribs 8 through 10 connect to the ribs above them via cartilage. The bottom ribs (11 and 12) float, ending at the sides of the torso, and not connecting to other bone or cartilage in front. The collar bone (clavicle) connects at the upper portion of the breastbone and the top, outer edge of the shoulder blade. The *pelvis* is a complex of several bones forming the structural base of the lower torso (Figure 2–1). The base of the spine (sacrum) forms the central

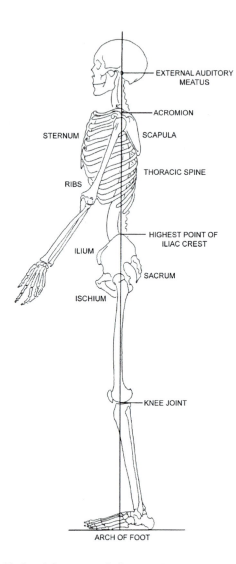

Figure 2–1 Skeletal framework for respiration, neutral posture
From M. B. Dayme (2009, 58).

portion of the pelvis in back. The two large bones on each side of the sacrum (left and right) making up most of the bowl shape of the pelvis are called the *ilia*. The bony structure you can press

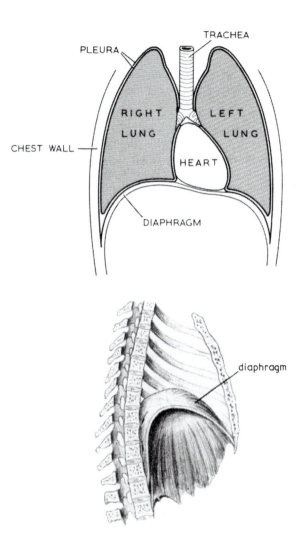

Figure 2–2 Position of the diaphragm
From M. B. Dayme (2009, 70–71).

against through soft tissue at the front, side, and back of your lower torso is the iliac crest, or the upper rim of the ilium bone. The pubic bone is located in the front of the pelvis and forms the front of the bowl shape of the pelvis. The bone forming the bottom of the pelvis is the *ischium*. The lower edge of the ischium bone, also called the *ischial tuberosity*, is the sit bone that you can feel pressing against the surface you're sitting on when you are sitting up straight.

MUSCLES OF BREATHING

The muscles of breathing can be divided into two groups: those that increase the size of the lungs for inhalation and those that decrease the size of the lungs for exhalation.

Inhalation Muscles The major muscles of inhalation are the diaphragm and the external intercostals. For rest breathing and quiet conversation, these muscles usually do all the work. The *diaphragm* is the large muscle that separates the contents of the thorax from those of the abdomen. The lungs and heart lie above the diaphragm, while the stomach, digestive system and other organs in the abdominal cavity lie below it (Figures 2–2 and 2–3).

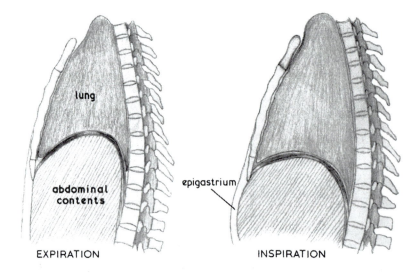

Figure 2–3 Movement of the abdominal contents: Expiration and inspiration From M. B. Dayme (2009, 72).

In its relaxed state, the diaphragm looks like an asymmetrical, upside-down bowl. When it contracts, it flattens and moves downward, pulling the bottom of the lungs (downward) with it (Figure 2–3). This increases the vertical dimension of the thoracic cavity, allowing the lungs to increase in size and pull breath in. This same motion—flattening of the diaphragm and increasing the size of the thorax—simultaneously pushes down on the contents of the abdomen. The stomach and other abdominal contents have to go somewhere, usually outward. If you don't otherwise constrict the abdomen, it will expand outward during a moderate to deep inhalation. The greatest increase in lung size, and therefore the deepest inhalations, occur when you allow the diaphragm to contract fully: This means *allowing* your stomach and lower abdomen to release outward. Holding in your stomach area by tensing abdominal muscles during inhalation prevents the diaphragm from moving freely to optimally expand the lungs. Holding in actually pushes the contents of the abdomen up against the underside of the diaphragm so that it can't contract and pull breath into the lungs. The diaphragm and abdominal muscles work in opposition to each other (antagonistic muscles). Dancers face a unique dilemma because they need to exchange a lot of air to obtain oxygen levels adequate for intense physical movement, yet may be trained to hold in their abdomen for balance, postural stability, and visual line. Their only option is to take frequent and relatively shallow breaths, allowing the rib cage to expand as much as it can.

The external intercostals are muscles that connect each rib to the neighboring rib below (Figure 2–4). Their fibers run diagonally, the direction of the tilt going from the sides of the body toward the front of the body as the fibers travel down to the next lower rib. The fibers are also more external (closer to the surface of the body) than the internal intercostals, which are exhalatory muscles. When the external intercostals contract, each rib pulls up on the rib below. Because of the curved shape of the ribs from front to back, raising the ribs together creates a larger space within the rib cage.

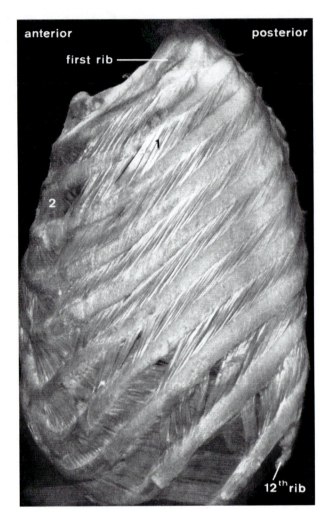

anterior   posterior

first rib ————

12thrib

Figure 2–4 Intercostal muscles From M. B. Dayme (2009, 76).

When the diaphragm and external intercostals both contract, a three-dimensional increase in volume inside the thorax occurs, consisting of an expansion toward the side, considerable front–back expansion, and limited vertical extension as well. The larger movements you sense during moderately deep inhalations will be overall expansion of the abdomen, as well as forward and side expansion of the rib cage. When very large inhalations are required, other accessory muscles can increase the size of the upper thorax in front by pulling the breastbone forward and upward (sternocleidomastoid), and the uppermost ribs upward and outward (pectoralis major, pectoralis minor, scalenes, subclavius, serratus anterior, and serratus posterior superior). You may also sense a feeling of expansion in the back and lower rib area.

Exhalation Muscles The most important muscles for exhalation are the abdominal muscles: rectus abdominis, external oblique, internal oblique, transverse abdominis (Figures 2–5 and 2–6).

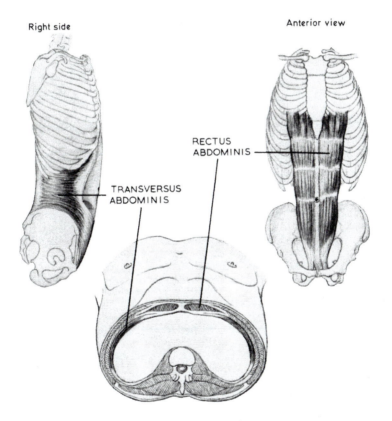

Figure 2–5 Abdominal muscles: Transversus abdominis, rectus abdominis From M. B. Dayme (2009, 82).

The rectus abdominis muscle fibers run vertically, the external and internal obliques fibers diagonally, and the transverse abdominis fibers wrap around the abdomen sideways. As a group, these muscles, which surround the contents of the abdomen, compress the contents upward and inward. This, in turn, exerts an upward pressure on the bottom of the lungs, compressing the lungs so that air can be exhaled. Other muscles can assist in further reducing the space surrounding the lungs by pulling the ribs downward. The internal intercostals (Figure 2–4), which are positioned deeper than the external intercostals (closer to the

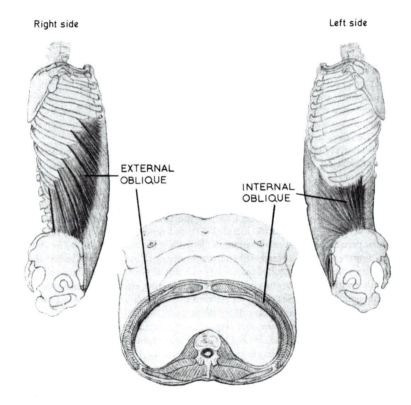

Figure 2–6 Abdominal muscles: External and internal obliques From M. B. Dayme (2009, 81).

inside of the body), are not as extensive or as strong as the external intercostals. The fibers of the internal intercostals run diagonally, the direction of the tilt going from the sides of the body to the midline of the body as the fibers travel upward from each rib to the next higher rib. They assist in pulling the ribs downward during exhalation. The transverse thoracis, serratus posterior inferior, and subcostals can also help pull down on the ribs. These actions decrease the size of the thorax; squeeze on the lungs; and, thus, help expel more air.

POSTURE AND BREATH SUPPORT

When you inhale, air flows through the nose and/or mouth, through the back of your throat (pharynx), through the open vocal folds in the larynx, and through the trachea (Figure 2–7). From there, the air flow is divided between the two bronchial tubes and into the right or left lobe of the lungs. The lungs occupy most of the inner space of the thorax, with one of the two lobes on each side of the heart. The tissue that forms the lungs is porous and very elastic. It allows the lungs to work like a sponge, but in *two* directions. A normal sponge can be compressed from its original size (its neutral condition) to a *smaller* size, and its elastic nature allows it to spring back to its original size. The lungs can go from their neutral condition (easy rest breathing) to a *larger* size for larger inhalations (increased physical activity or to supply air for a long sung or spoken phrase) and back to neutral. If more exhaled breath is needed, however, lung tissue can be squeezed from its neutral size to a *smaller* size.

Between the outer surface of the lungs (the visceral pleura) and inner walls of the thorax (the parietal pleura), there is a thin liquid-filled space (the pleural cavity) that keeps them linked, much like two plates stuck together with water between them (Figure 2–2). When the ribs move upward and outward and the diaphragm contracts and descends, the overall size of the thorax increases. Because the surface of the lungs adheres to the inside of the ribs and the top surface of the diaphragm, the size of the

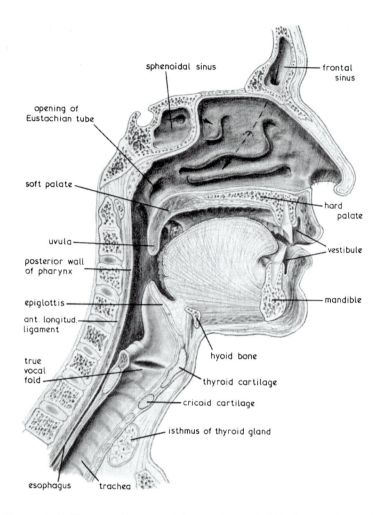

Figure 2–7 The vocal tract and larynx From M. B. Dayme (2009, 92).

lungs increases along with the thorax (inhalation). When the abdominal muscles pull the content of the abdomen inward and upward against the relaxed diaphragm, and the ribs move downward and inward, the opposite happens—with inward pressure on the thorax from all directions, the thorax shrinks in size and old air is squeezed out of the spongy lungs (exhalation).

Optimal breathing for speech and singing occurs when body position and posture allow for large inhalations and exhalations to occur. Large breath volumes occur when the volume of the thorax is relatively large, and there is no postural compression of the abdomen or rib cage. This occurs when posture is relatively neutral or balanced (Figure 2–1). Body weight is centered both left/right and front/back. For most of us, this will create a *plumb-line* alignment with the opening of the ear (external auditory meatus), the upper/outer point of the shoulder blade (acromion), the sides of your hip bone (highest point of the iliac crest), the knee joint, and the arch of the feet vertically in line.

In your current voice production, you may notice that you *grab*, or gasp, for air when you want a larger inhalation. The gasping sound occurs if you constrict your vocal folds during inhalation. In other words, you're *blocking* the inward flow of the air you want if the inhalation is noisy. Letting go of this habit means being able to clearly distinguish between the sensation of muscular tensions inside the neck constricting your larynx and pharynx during gaspy inhalations and the different body sensations during quick, deep, and free inhalations. The ability to draw in quiet, deep inhalations will supply you with the flow of air you need to support your speech and singing.

Support is a term that is applied to different phenomena by different people. This inconsistent usage makes it difficult to describe what a specific coach or teacher may mean by it. In physiological terms, support might simply be described as providing flexible, optimal levels of breath flow to the vocal folds so that they can produce healthy and vibrant vocal sounds. If there's not enough breath stream for the sound you intend, you may end up compensating by squeezing the vocal folds to create more pressure. Good support means less risk for pressure injuries to the vocal folds due to such compensatory squeezing. On the other hand, going to the other extreme is not optimal. If you overblow, or *push*, the breath, you may end up creating a vocal timbre that is poorer than what you intend.

Phonation

Phonation is the formal term used to refer to sound production in the larynx. The larynx is a soft tissue tube, albeit a complex one, that connects the pharynx with the trachea (Figure 2–7). Although most of us think of the larynx as the origin of voice, its primary biological role is to protect the upper airway (nose, mouth, pharynx) and lungs from blockage. If our access to air is blocked off, oxygen flow to the body stops and serious brain damage or death can occur. The larynx allows us to unblock the airway by coughing. Within the larynx, the vocal folds operate like a valve, shutting off or turning on various amounts of exhaled air at various pressures, that pass through the upper airway. When you cough, the vocal folds shut tightly, so that air pressure can get built up in the lungs beneath them, and then suddenly release. This sudden release of the air pressure (upward/outward) dislodges foreign material in the airway. Whenever you swallow, your vocal folds close tightly to protect your airway as food goes into the esophagus (food tube). The esophagus is behind the larynx (they share a common wall) and in front of your cervical vertebrae.

The larynx's secondary role is serving as the source of sound for speech and singing. The vocal folds interact with the airstream to produce a vocal buzz at different pitches, loudness levels, and vocal registers, as well as different kinds of whispers.

FRAMEWORK

The muscles and soft tissue of the larynx, including the vocal folds, are attached to bone or cartilage. The shapes of the bone and cartilage, and the location of the joints connecting them to one another, define the relationships among the muscles and define the range of the movements in the larynx (e.g., opening and closing the vocal folds, stretching the vocal folds, thinning out or bulking up the vocal folds). The bony/cartilaginous framework is composed of one bone (the hyoid bone) and several cartilages (Figure 2–8). The hyoid (meaning U-shaped) bone is shared, in the sense that it is the uppermost hard struc-

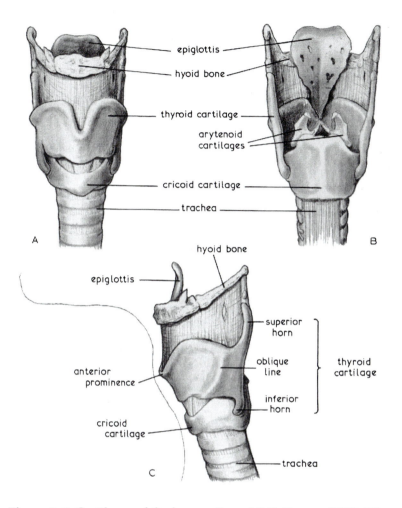

Figure 2–8 Cartilages of the larynx From M. B. Dayme (2009, 94).

ture of the larynx, but is also the bone in the root of the tongue (Figure 2–7). Any motion of the tongue that causes the hyoid bone to be pulled up or forward will, therefore, also pull the larynx upward. When you swallow, notice how the body of your tongue moves forward in your mouth then back down to its normal position. Swallow again, and notice how your Adam's apple—the part of the larynx protruding forward in your neck—moves up and down in tandem. These are reflexive, or automatically programmed movements, that occur every time you swallow.

There are three single cartilages—the epiglottis, the thyroid, and the cricoid—and three paired cartilages—the arytenoids, the corniculates, and the cuneiforms. The cartilages are structurally firm but somewhat softer and more pliable than bone. When we're infants, they are much more flexible, but as we age they become more bonelike (ossification—more rigid and calcified). The epiglottis is a large leaf-shaped cartilage in the upper part of the larynx right behind the hyoid bone (Figure 2–8). It serves as additional protection during swallowing, functioning like an extra door to seal off the airway below. This prevents fluid or food material from getting into the lungs.

The thyroid cartilage serves as a shield in front of the vocal folds (Figures 2–7 and 2–8). It is folded in the center so that the sides of the vocal folds are also protected. The angle of the fold is what protrudes from the neck as the Adam's apple. In women, the vocal folds are less long, front to back, which results in less of a thyroid protrusion forward in the neck (Figures 2–9a and 2–9b). The cricoid cartilage is at the lowest part of the larynx tube and connects with the beginning of the trachea (Figure 2–8). The arytenoids are the pair of cartilages that sit on the back upper rim of the cricoid cartilage. They are the cartilages that allow for vocal fold movement because they serve as the back attachment for the left and right vocal folds. Their position determines the degree to which the larynx is open (e.g., for air exchange) or closed (e.g., for voicing or airway protection). A number of muscles within the larynx control this movement of the arytenoid cartilages. The other paired cartilages (corniculates and cuneiforms) are not directly involved in vocal production.

MUSCLES

Vocal fold opening (abduction) is controlled by the posterior cricoarytenoid muscle. When it contracts, it makes the arytenoid on each side swivel atop the cricoid in such a way that the front end

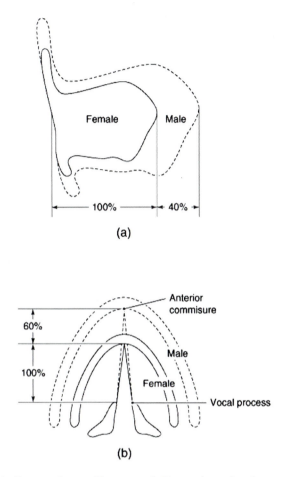

Figure 2–9 Comparison of laryngeal dimensions for the male versus the female larynx: (a) thyroid cartilage, and (b) membranous vocal fold length From I. R. Titze (2000, 179). Copyright 2000, National Center for Voice and Speech.

of the arytenoid, that's attached to the back of the vocal fold on each side, gets swung out from the midline of the body toward the side, creating a sort of triangular opening for breathing (Figure 2–10). Three muscles can help close the vocal folds (adduction) in different ways. The lateral cricoarytenoid is the

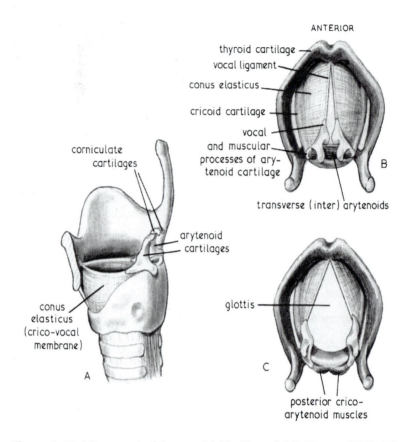

Figure 2–10 Movement of the vocal folds From M. B. Dayme (2009, 97).

antagonistic muscle to the posterior cricoarytenoid mentioned previously. When the lateral cricoarytenoid contracts, it makes the front end of each arytenoid (attached to vocal fold) swivel from the sides toward the midline of the body, effectively closing the vocal folds together. When you really need a very tight seal between the vocal folds, the thyroarytenoid muscles, which are inside and form the bulk of the vocal folds themselves, can contract. This bulks up the vocal folds and makes their inner edges lean more against each other. The back part of the opening between vocal folds (between the arytenoid cartilages) can form a small air flow leak unless the arytenoids push together. Contraction of the interarytenoid muscles closes off this small leak space. (You can speak or sing with this leak—it doesn't let significant amounts of air escape. Many women and soft-spoken men have their vocal folds in this configuration when they speak, which tends to make the voice less brilliant or harsh in timbre.) This leak space closure happens reflexively when you need airway protection, for holding your breath, or for speaking with a loud, strong voice.

Pitch is actively raised when the cricothyroid muscle is contracted. When this happens, the bottom of the thyroid cartilage and the top of the cricoid cartilage are moved closer together, and the thyroid cartilage gets pulled forward. Since the front ends of the vocal folds are attached to the inside of the fold of the thyroid cartilage, the vocal folds get pulled along with the thyroid cartilage. This pulling forward of the vocal folds stretches out and thins them, and your pitch goes up. This phenomenon is similar to what happens to a guitar string as you turn the peg clockwise. As the end of the string (attached to the peg) gets pulled/wound up, the string becomes thinner and more taut, which makes its pitch go up.

Put your fingertips on your Adam's (or Eve's) apple and notice what happens when you make a comfortable pitch and move up one step or one half-step on the scale. Most of us will sense a slight forward protrusion of the thyroid and maybe a little downward tilting. Do this again for an octave glide. Slide up and down the scale, and see if the larynx moves up or down within your neck. The upper strap muscles (Figure 2–11) often assist in pitch-raising in singers and speakers who have not worked on stabilizing the larynx's position in the neck. In other words, unless you work to deactivate the upper strap muscles during pitch-raising to keep your larynx in a neutral position for higher pitches, you'll get an accompanying shortening of the vocal tract. This can give your singing a squeezed, or yelping, kind of timbre.

The vocal folds make it possible to have an incredible variety of vocal "colors," to a large degree by their design. There are three anatomical layers in each vocal fold: a thin, but very pliable

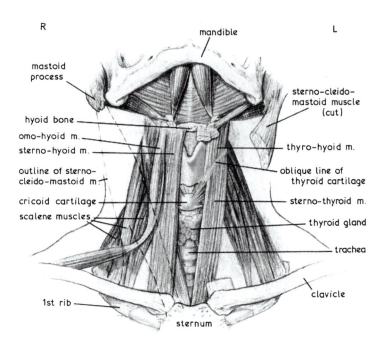

R

mandible

L

mastoid
process

sterno–cleido–
mastoid muscle
(cut)

hyoid bone

omo–hyoid m.

sterno–hyoid m.

thyro–hyoid m.

outline of sterno–
cleido–mastoid m.

oblique line of
thyroid cartilage

cricoid cartilage

sterno–thyroid m.

scalene muscles

thyroid gland

trachea

clavicle

1st rib

sternum

Figure 2–11 Strap muscles From M. B. Dayme (2009, 101).

protective layer called the mucosa; a somewhat less flexible, but more stable layer called the vocal ligament, which provides structural integrity; and the inner filling, or muscle tissue (the thyroarytenoid). It is the highly elastic and flexible mucosa that is crucial to production of a smooth, clear voice. This top layer is where most of the movement in vocal fold vibration occurs.

I've described how the vocal folds can be stretched along their length to raise pitch, like strings on a stringed instrument. How is it that *one* set of vocal strings can create such a large pitch range? One reason is that we can phonate in more than one register. Although the number and size of vocal registers is an ongoing point of debate in music, the linguistic, medical, and voice therapy communities talk about three basic ones: glottal fry (also called creaky voice or pulse register), chest (also called modal), and falsetto (also called loft). The terms in parentheses are some-times used by therapists and researchers. It is practical to think of registers as different thickness settings of the vocal folds. Glot-tal fry can be produced for low tones when the vocal folds are thick and loose. If glottal fry is done without excessive tension, it is not harmful as such. It can end up happening at the ends of phrases that are produced with very little energy. Although glot-tal fry may not be harmful to the voice per se, it is rarely useful in vocal performance.

Most of us vocalize for speech and singing in chest or fal-setto registers. Chest register voicing is what most of us use for conversational speech and low to mid-upper range singing. In chest register, the vocal folds are relatively thick and taut; the muscles inside the vocal folds, the thyroarytenoids (TA for short), are contracted, which bulks up/firms up the vocal folds. Falsetto register voicing can be used for the upper-middle to top-most pitches. In falsetto register, there is little or no contraction of the thyroarytenoid, so the folds are thinner and less bulky. Only the surface mucosa of the vocal folds vibrates.

In both chest and falsetto registers, the freedom and sym-metry of the vibration of the mucosa is of the utmost importance for keeping your vocal quality intact. Any use of the vocal folds that damages the mucosa will reduce its pliability and elasticity, and, in turn, the symmetry of the vocal fold vibration. In practi-cal terms, this means taking off top notes from your pitch range and losing the smooth quality of the high pitches you have left.

Earlier, when I described how the vocal folds close, I men-tioned different *degrees* of how tightly the vocal folds could be closed. It is this continuum of how tightly the vocal folds are closed/squeezed that gives us yet another dimension of vocal quality: from breathy voice to normal voice to pressed voice. You can explore this by making long tones transitioning from your habitual vocal sound to a sound that is gradually more and more breathy, or from your habitual vocal sounds to a more squeezed or choked sound. Some of us who don't use enough breath flow in our habitual voices tend to compensate by squeezing with the vocal folds to get a normal vocal volume. If you take this kind of partially squeezed sound louder (what most untrained people do) when you need to be heard over a distance or over noise, you significantly increase your risk for pressure injuries to the mucosa of the vocal folds—swelling in the vocal folds, vocal fatigue, and hoarseness.

LOUDNESS CONTROL

There is widespread agreement among voice researchers that the source of increased vocal intensity or loudness is an increase in air pressure beneath the vocal folds (i.e., subglottal pressure or lung pressure). If you've ever watched a film or video of vocal fold movement during vocalization, you've probably noticed that for soft sounds the extent of vocal fold movement outward and inward (amplitude of vibration) is small. The vocal folds either collide gently or just barely touch. As louder and louder sounds are made, movement of the vocal folds becomes wider and their collisions harder. The more pressure blowing open the vocal folds during each cycle of vibration, the wider the folds swing out. The wider they swing out, the stronger the sound is when they clap together.

Two mechanisms are used to increase subglottal pressure, and they usually work together: (1) increasing airflow and (2) increasing compression of the vocal folds. The basic physical principle that applies for all fluids (liquids and gases alike) can be summarized in the following relationship:

Pressure = Flow × Resistance

Let me use an analogy to illustrate the relationship: getting more water pressure out of a garden hose. Let's say you've turned the faucet enough so that you have enough water pressure to water some nearby flowers gently. You've finished and now want to water a patch of lawn fifteen feet away but don't want to walk over there. How can you get more water *pressure* so that the spray will hit that area? Two ways: You can put your thumb over part of the opening of the hose (i.e., increase *resistance* to the existing water flow), or you can go and turn the faucet to increase the water *flow*. In both cases, you get an increased amount of water pressure so that you can spray further. Realistically, when using a garden hose you would probably use a combination of both.

The same relationship holds for creating the breath energy (subglottal pressure) needed for vocalization. Your healthiest loud voice is going to be produced with ample breath flow. A loud voice created with ample breath flow produces much less risk for injury than a loud voice created by poor breath flow and compensatory pressing of the vocal folds. In other words, when you're stingy with your breath flow, you end up putting excessive pressure on your vocal folds, which can lead to vocal fold damage (e.g., nodules, polyps).

Articulation

Articulation is the movement of the articulators (tongue, teeth, lips, jaws, and soft palate) that create speech sounds. Speech sounds occur because these movements change the shape of the vocal tract (the tube formed by the soft tissue from just above your larynx, through your pharynx and oral cavity, ending at your lips). Every speech sound is created by a specific configuration of vocal tract length and shape (Figure 2–12).

Arthur Lessac, a noted voice trainer, compares each speech sound to a specific musical instrument. His metaphor is right on target because each vocal tract configuration acts like a differently shaped resonating cavity. Words can be thought of as sounds created by the movements between several vocal tract shapes, strung together in a sequence. The vocal tract shapes resonate the vocal buzz of the larynx to create the differences in sound quality and allow us to distinguish one vowel from another and one consonant from another. The buzz sound from the larynx is literally bounced around (resonated) in the vocal

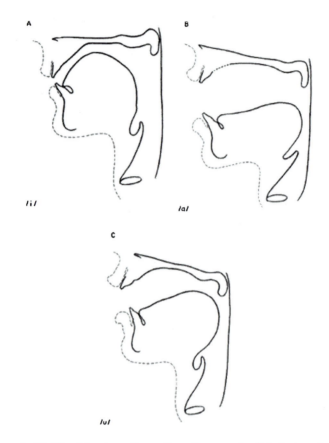

Figure 2–12 Vocal tract configurations for vowels /i/, /ɑ/, and /u/— tracings from X-ray images From M. B. Dayme (2009, 134).

tract. The buzz is composed of a family of related sound frequencies called *overtones*, or *harmonics*. Resonation modifies the vocal buzz in such a way that some of its overtones are more heavily damped (muffled) than others. Depending on the vocal tract's length and shape, the strength of some overtones is reduced and other overtones are favored.

An analogy that helps me think about the functional relationship between the buzz and the vocal tract is the relationship between clay and molds for shaping clay into different figurines.

If you think of vocal buzz as the *clay* (the core material of your sound), each shape your vocal tract makes is like a *mold* that shapes the clay into a recognizable entity. In speaking and singing, you can create a multitude of vocal tract length and shape configurations, which modify the basic buzz sound into a huge palette of linguistically and emotionally meaningful vocal qualities. In using *vocal quality* here, I refer not only to perceivable differences in consonant and vowel identity, but also to your individual voice timbre, which allows people to recognize you when you speak.

Notice the close proximity and interconnectedness of the anatomical structures of the larynx and vocal tract (Figure 2–7). The tongue is anchored to the hyoid bone at its base. Because of this design, articulation of vowels and consonants that require the body of the tongue to move forward pull the hyoid forward. The hyoid is also the top of the larynx, so every forward movement of the tongue can pull your larynx up with it unless you compensate by releasing the jaw. This will give you a squeezed, yelping kind of vocal timbre that is associated with a tense, high larynx. If you release your jaw during such articulatory gestures, letting it relax down and toward your neck, you allow the larynx to remain in a more neutral position. When your larynx can work in a more neutral position, and the vocal tract is freer of extraneous tension, your spoken/sung text will sound freer and more vibrant.

Sensation and Learning

The initiation of any spoken or sung communication is the *intention* to express a message aloud. The message may be a response to something you hear, or to something you're thinking or feeling. As you mentally form or recall your idea, the following series of mental and physical events occur in rapid succession making vocalization possible.

1. The language areas of your brain select and then sequence *words and phrases* that describe your thought.

2. The language areas of your brain select and sequence the *sounds* that make up a phrase or sentence.

3. The motor area of your brain sends a precisely sequenced and coordinated series of *commands to the muscles* of the respiratory system, the larynx, and the articulators to produce the sounds.

When you start a vocal sound or phrase, you've inhaled an amount of breath that is usually enough to provide airflow to produce the first phrase or group of related words. The clearer your intention is (i.e., the clearer the words, sounds, and emotions are in your mind), the better the part of the brain controlling the respiratory system can gauge how much air it needs and the speed and intensity of respiratory muscle activity that needs to occur to get that air in before you speak. Once you're into the phrase, all three mechanisms work in synchrony, and any imbalance or weakness in one mechanism can create compensatory actions in another.

On a physical level, we do not have complete volitional control over all aspects of vocal production (nor do you want to be focusing on it when you're performing). However, to the degree to which we can access *sensations* related to what occurs in the body systems that produce voice, we do have some direct and indirect control of the physical processes. These may include sensations of contraction or stretch in muscles, skin, and other soft tissue; sensation of degree of joint movement; as well as sensations of sympathetic vibration in bony or soft structures of the face, neck, or chest. Acquiring a technique relies on focusing attention on *differences* in these sensations as you produce different types or qualities of sound. Awareness of these sensations serves as your most reliable guide by, in a sense, *measuring* what you're doing physically as you explore vocally and make choices in the process of solidifying your technique. In this aspect, training the voice is very similar to training in other complex physical motor tasks: dancing, playing a sport, playing a musical instrument.

One reason body sensations are relied on as the primary sensory feedback in vocal training is that perception of your own voice is not always reliable feedback. The acoustics of different performance spaces can significantly change the sound of your voice. More important, however, is the fact that you hear your voice different from the way others do. When you *hear* yourself, your hearing mechanism gets both air-conducted sound (from the room) and bone-conducted sound (from bone vibration in the skull during vocalization). Some of the low frequencies of the vocal buzz you make in your larynx get conducted by the bones but don't make it out into the room. This makes the sound of your voice *fuller*, or more powerful, to you as compared to a high-fidelity recording of your voice. Listeners in the room (and audio-recording equipment) can only pick up the air-conducted sound.

Vocal Health and Longevity

Your lungs, your vocal folds, and your articulators are necessarily robust under normal conditions. In their primary biological roles, they allow you to take in the breath of life (literally), keep you from choking when you eat, and let you chew and process the food and liquid you need to stay alive. For most people in good health, the demands of day-to-day conversations tend to be taken in stride by the tissues of the vocal folds. It can be a different story for performers who use their voices much more extensively, both in terms of vocal variety and amount of talking/singing time per day. The additional demands of performing can increase the risk of vocal fold inflammation (swelling) from overuse (i.e., more use than your vocal folds can tolerate with your current technique).

Think about what happens when surface tissue on your fingertips gets stressed from repeated pressure against them (e.g., pressing down on guitar strings repetitively several hours a day). Your skin and the tissues just beneath it get injured from the pressure of the movements. The first tissue-injury response you get is a blister or localized swelling. The swelling is part of the healing response and helps remove injured/dead tissue cells.

If you press on a blistered fingertip repeatedly, you'll eventually get a callous—abnormally hard tissue growth—at the injury site as a long-term protective response.

During normal phonation, the vocal folds collide, pressing against each other, often hundreds of times or more per second. If phonation is intermittent and not loud, as it is for most nonprofessional voice use, any minor swelling due to the force of these collisions has a chance to resolve fairly quickly. If extensive heavy use of the voice (loud voice, greater use of the extremes of pitch range, especially high pitches) is added to normal voice use without adequate time for healing, vocal fold swelling may not have a chance to resolve. A vicious cycle can begin: You may notice you have to work harder to produce voice, you can't speak softly without voice breaks, your high pitches are harder to produce or gone, your voice seems lower in pitch, or your voice is hoarse or unclear. So, you may try to compensate by pushing your voice.

Swollen vocal folds, because they are water-logged and heavier, are harder to set into motion (i.e., higher subglottal pressures are required to get them vibrating and to keep them going). The higher the subglottal pressure, the greater the pressure force is between the vocal folds as they strike each other. Any efforts to compensate by pushing with force of breath can aggravate the already swollen vocal folds even further. If you also push with more muscular effort by squeezing the vocal folds tighter (pressed voice or hyperadduction), this exacerbates a pressure-induced injury. Many physicians and voice therapists call this *phonotrauma*, or trauma to the tissues of the vocal folds, caused by how vocal sound has been produced. Regardless of why your vocal folds are swollen, whether it's due to pressure-related injury or a viral or bacterial infection, you need to allow them to heal.

Chronic, high-demand use of swollen vocal folds can lead to higher risk of permanent tissue damage such as vocal nodules or polyps. It's important, therefore, to reduce risk for injury to the vocal folds. There are several ways to do this. A healthy, reliable technique for producing high-risk voice (loud, extreme pitches, extensive use) and an awareness of your vocal health are your best tools to keep the expressive range of your voice intact for years to come. Laryngologists (ear, nose, throat physicians), who specialize in health of the larynx, and voice therapists (speech-language pathologists), who specialize in working with voice disorders, also stress the importance of good vocal hygiene in keeping the vocal folds healthy and reducing the risk of permanent injury.

VOCAL HYGIENE SUGGESTIONS

Reducing Risk for Tissue Injury

1. Hydrate adequately. For an average adult, a good goal for water consumption is eight glasses (64 oz.) of water per day. Noncaffeinated fluids count, but water is preferable. Adequate systemic (whole body) hydration helps keep the cells of vocal fold tissues pliable, allowing the vocal folds to vibrate with less breath pressure (especially for high pitches). Good hydration also reduces the thickness/stickiness of the mucus that cleans and lubricates the lining of the respiratory system. This mucus is normally so thin in texture that it's not noticed. The presence of thick nasal mucus and/or postnasal drip usually occurs when the normally thin mucus is thick with dead cells/debris, which it carries away from these areas during a viral or bacterial infection. In this case, it's not the mucus that's the problem, it's the fact that you've got a cold. Drinking lots of fluids is recommended during colds because fluids help to thin out these secretions, thus allowing dead cells/tissue debris to be carried away more effectively so that you can heal faster. Taking a plain expectorant containing guaifenesin (e.g., Mucinex or plain Robitussin without any cough suppressants) can also help to thin out secretions.

2. If you live or work in a dry, dusty, or overheated area, breathe through your nose as much as possible. The nose filters, humidifies, and warms the air you inhale, so it's

freer of particulates and moister and warmer when it arrives in your lungs. Breathing through your mouth tends to dry out your mouth, throat, and vocal folds more quickly than nasal breathing. In the process of vocal training and in performance, however, mouth breathing is fine; in fact, it's necessary to allow deep, quick inhalations.

3. When the humidity level is low (30 percent or less) or when you are congested, using a warm-air humidifier and/or steam treatments can soothe and moisten irritated or swollen nose, sinus, and throat areas.

4. When taking over-the-counter and/or prescription medications that are dehydrating to the body, compensate with increased hydration. Many drugstore remedies for colds or allergies (e.g., decongestants or antihistamines) are dehydrating. Prescription antihistamines tend to be less so.

5. Reduce caffeine and alcohol consumption. Both caffeine and alcohol are dehydrating. The dehydration effect is intensified when you are in very low-humidity environments (including airplane cabins). Alcohol and caffeine also exacerbate heartburn. Chronic heartburn, also known as Gastroesophageal Reflux Disease (GERD) or Laryngopharyngeal Reflux Disease, can occur when acid from the stomach backs up into the esophagus and throat. When the sphincter muscle at the entrance to the stomach doesn't close off completely, the acidic digestive fluid from the stomach (hydrochloric acid) can back up or reflux into the esophagus or further up into the back of the larynx/vocal folds. Alcohol and caffeine tend to loosen the sphincter muscle. Refluxed acid from the stomach can irritate the back of the vocal folds causing them to swell and redden. Reflux of stomach acid on the vocal folds can occur without obvious heartburn symptoms/sensations, especially during sleep when gravity doesn't help to keep the stomach acid down.

6. Eat your last meal of the day three or more hours before you go to sleep. This suggestion is also related to reflux of stomach acid. If you don't give your digestive system adequate time to digest your last meal of the day, you end up lying flat while the stomach is full and churning away with acidic stomach fluid trying to break down your meal. If your stomach is relatively full, the pressure from your stomach's contents pushing against the seal between the stomach and the esophagus makes it easier for reflux to occur and for it to travel to the larynx. This type of irritation can cause subtle, or not so subtle, changes in your voice production—your voice may tire/fatigue more easily and high pitches may become difficult or seemingly impossible to produce.

Minimizing Trauma

1. Do not smoke and avoid second-hand smoke; at the very least, try to limit your exposure. Smoking is considered chemical trauma to the vocal folds and the airway in general. Heavy, continuous smoking can cause permanent swelling of the vocal folds and deformation of the surface of the vocal folds (polypoid degeneration) and related losses of pitch and loudness range and smooth vocal quality.

2. Conserve your voice, when you can. Limit the amount of time you have to talk over noise (e.g., over machine or engine noise) or in loud, crowded rooms.

3. Avoid prolonged periods of high-stress vocalization: very loud talking, singing, screaming, shouting. When you have used your voice strenuously, promote tissue recovery by resting the voice as soon as possible. Even a few minutes helps.

4. Avoid *harsh* glottal attacks. If it's a habit, work on eradicating the harshness. One of the unspoken rules of English pronunciation we acquire as native speakers is

to produce stressed, vowel-initiated syllables (e.g., open, aptitude, every) with a glottal onset or *attack*. To produce this slight click or popping sound that we're used to hearing and feeling at the beginning of the vowel, the vocal folds fully close momentarily just before the vowel, then open as the vowel is initiated. In a harsh glottal attack, the vocal folds strike each other with considerable force several times, which can contribute to the overall load of pressure injury risks.

5. Take steps to reduce chronic coughing or throat clearing. The vocal folds strike each other repeatedly and with great force (much greater than during most speech/singing) during coughing or throat clearing and can add to the overall load of pressure injury risk. Find out what is causing the habitual coughing or throat clearing and take care of it. The solution may be as simple as drinking more water if the source of the cough is postnasal drip or thick secretions stuck in your throat. A cough that lasts for more than a few weeks is not normal and could be a symptom of something more serious.

6. Limit the amount of talking/singing during colds or other respiratory conditions if there is vocal fold inflammation. Swollen vocal folds are at higher risk of injury to the pliable surface tissue, which is more stretched out and vulnerable than healthy tissue. Think of how the surface of a water balloon is more vulnerable to puncture/breakage when it is very full.

7. Avoid using a forced stage whisper; soft breathy voice actually produces less strain. When you produce a forced stage whisper, you force a very high-pressure airstream through a small opening in the back of the vocal folds (between the arytenoid cartilages). The high-pressure airstream creates turbulence noise that forms the whisper. To resist the high pressure beneath them, the front portions of the vocal folds are pressed together firmly

and end up rubbing against each other, creating friction between them. If you have a cold, it is less stressful on the vocal folds to use a soft and slightly breathy phonation for conversation and rehearsal than to use a stage whisper. If you have to produce a stage whisper for a performance, just remember to rest your voice as soon as possible.

8. If you are a heavy voice user, establish a daily routine of warm-up and cool-down. A progressive vocal warm-up brings blood and oxygen gradually to the muscles of breathing and phonation, and it is an opportunity to focus your awareness of the body sensations that guide your voice production. A warmed-up body (respiratory and phonatory systems included) is less prone to injury.

Immune System Health

1. Maintain overall good health: eat nutritionally rich foods, get effective rest and sleep, and nourish your body/mind with regular exercise and movement. The more nearly optimal your physical health is, the more optimally your immune system can respond to vocal fatigue or injury.

2. Provide for your emotional and spiritual needs. A life lived well is not only therapeutic, it brings you closer to the truth of who you are, which is ultimately the source of your creativity.

References

Dayme, M. B. 2009. *Dynamics of the Singing Voice* (5th ed.). New York: Springer-Verlag Wien.

Titze, I. R. 1994. *Principles of Voice Production*. Englewood Cliffs, NJ: Prentice-Hall, Inc.; Second printing ©2000, National Center for Voice and Speech, Iowa City, IA.

Suggested Reading

Denes, P. B., and Pinson, E. N. 1993. *The Speech Chain: The Physics and Biology of Spoken Language* (2nd edition). New York: W. H. Freeman.

Hixon, T. J. 1987. *Respiratory Function in Speech and Song.* San Diego: Singular Publishing Group.

Netter, F. H. 2010. *Atlas of Human Anatomy* (5th ed.). Philadelphia: Saunders.

Zemlin, W. R. 1998. *Speech and Hearing Science. Anatomy and Physiology* (4th ed.). Englewood Cliffs, NJ: Prentice-Hall.

Internet Resources

The Larynx and Voice Surgery, University of Iowa Medical Center—*www.medicine.uiowa.edu/otolaryngology/cases.*

Center for Voice and Swallowing, UC Davis Health System—*www.ucdvoice.org.*

The National Center for Voice and Speech—*www.ncvs.org.*

3 ■ Range, Resonance, and Articulation

Overview

Although it is convenient to separate vocal technique into its several elements for purposes of discussion, every aspect of voice use directly or indirectly affects the whole mechanism. For example, alignment and breathing are integrally connected to the performer's range, resonance, and articulation. Likewise, articulation, or the shaping of sound through manipulation of the vocal tract, has a profound effect on the quality, or resonance, of that sound, as well as on the range of pitches that are readily available to the singer and actor.

In this chapter, you will find exercises designed to explore high and low pitches in a safe and playful manner. As you do those exercises, you may also discover resonance possibilities that are infinitely interesting, but not always *beautiful*. For the actor, any vocal utterance is potentially useful, and nontraditional sounds often tap into extraordinary possibilities for character development. Text, or even articulation drills, can be incorporated whenever they seem appropriate.

Extending the Range

It is the middle of the pitch range that must be solid, in speaking as well as singing, for the extremes are just that and tend to be more sparingly used than the midrange of a professional actor or singer. The midrange of an untrained voice is usually quite a different matter in that it tends to be both smaller and less consistent in quality than that of the trained voice user. Therefore basic work in theatre voice and singing often focuses on extending the boundaries of the untrained voice to meet the demands of professional material.

Extending the range is like building any other part of the body. It involves careful and conscious work to develop strength, stamina, and ease of production for a variety of tasks. Accents and dialects alone are sure to challenge the actor's range of pitch, color, and articulatory pattern, and virtually every production, musical and otherwise, is a *dialect show*, in other words (1) most events happen somewhere, and (2) attention to the details of a character's speech—spoken or sung—is an essential part of the actor's work.

EXERCISES

In this chapter, we will continue the physical/vocal work outlined in Chapter 1. Several of the exercises here are adapted from the Destructuring/Restructuring work of Catherine Fitzmaurice. *Destructuring* is intended to release the performer from habitual and often inefficient breathing patterns, while *Restructuring* consciously uses and deepens the pattern of breathing we normally observe in quiet, untutored rest.

Nodding the Head

Sit cross-legged on the floor (or you may do the exercise in virtually any position sitting or standing) with your sternum high and the back of your neck long and flexible. Find the *beginning* of a yawn in the back of your throat but keep your lips touching. Start with a comfortable low pitch and siren up (include falsetto) as you nod your head forward until it drops to your chest (Figure 3–1). In a continuous motion, return your head to upright, humming high to low, and so on, several times; smooth out the siren as you go. In this instance, being upright may mean that

Figure 3–1 Nodding the Head

your chin is a bit higher than neutral. This exercise can be done almost anywhere to (1) enlarge the resonating space, develop muscle tone in the pharynx and soft palate, and focus the tone so that it is clear, not breathy; (2) work through a large pitch range that is easily accessible because of the nodding of the head (high notes being easier in rounded positions); and (3) connect automatically with deep abdominal action that relates directly to the siren. You will probably notice more abdominal movement, inward and upward, as you go higher in pitch (nodding), and a release of that movement as you go down in pitch (moving to upright). You might think of the abdomen as the power source for the voice; once you're connected to that source, your body does what is required to produce the sounds you want! As you inhale (silently), you may observe considerable lateral and posterior expansion in your lower ribs, along with the letting go of your abdominal muscles. These actions in the middle and lower torso are essential elements in Restructuring the breath.

Plough Sequence

The first part of this sequence is taken directly from Catherine Fitzmaurice's Destructuring positions. The rest is my own adaptation of additional yoga-based postures and movement work from Annie Loui, Pilates, and Suzuki.

Lie on your back (or go into the Plough directly from the Dying Roach), then take your legs up to over your head. If you like, you can go into the full yoga Plough, then roll back and put the weight of your hips and buttocks in your hands—prop your arms at the elbows. Having your elbows on the floor can also help you to curl over easily. You must *put the weight* of the buttocks in your hands; otherwise your belly will not be free. If you take your hands away, your buttocks should fall to the floor.

1. Separate your legs and feet to about hip-width apart and allow your knees to fall toward your ears. This is the Resting position. If your breathing is deep, you should be very comfortable here and will probably notice considerable expansion and release in your middle and lower back. This position is not for all bodies, however, so if curling to this degree is difficult for you, simply modify the exercise or go on to the Shoulder Stand.

2. Begin to straighten your legs slightly, leading with your heels, and turn your toes inward (legs parallel to the floor). You will probably get a tremor in your legs. Enjoy it, and play with sounds if you like, especially high sounds. Don't go for full-voiced high Cs! What you'll probably have is just the edge of the tone, so staccatos will be great. This is the modified, or Half Plough, in the Fitzmaurice work (Figure 3–2).

Figure 3–2 The Half Plough

3. Now take your legs straight up, still keeping the weight of your buttocks in your hands. Again, turn your toes inward slightly and flex your feet, leading with your heels, to initiate a tremor (Figure 3–3). High sounds are easy in this position, which is a modified yoga Shoulder Stand. As a variation, reach for the tremor with your toes.

4. When you're ready, take your legs all the way over your head, toes on the floor, and take your arms back parallel to your legs to get a wonderful stretch. Your breath should be noticeably released and deep by now. This is the Full Plough.

5. Rounding your head *toward your chest*, come up slowly to a No Hands, No Feet position, balancing on your tailbone and lower buttocks. Be sure you are not straining in your upper chest and neck; ideally your sternum is high and your head and neck are free. Your abdominal and back muscles are working to maintain the position; however, a part of that network of protection and strength is available

Figure 3–3 Modified Shoulder Stand

for breath management and in this position your body iden-
tifies the distinctive role of each part of the musculature.

- Move your arms and legs smoothly and let your voice
  do whatever smooth sounds feel appropriate and fun.
- Flex your feet and press gently with the heels of your
  hands to initiate tremors in your legs and arms; use
  your voice.
- Bring your legs straight up in front of your face, or open
  them to a V, holding your ankles or legs with your hands
  and vocalize (e.g., lip and tongue trills in a variety of pat-

terns) and/or work on a Shakespeare sonnet, doing four lines per breath (until the couplet). This is a great way to feel expansion in your back on the inhalation, and you will notice definite and efficient abdominal action as you speak or sing on the exhalation. The physical shape is adapted from Pilates training (Figure 3–4).

- Straighten your legs out in front of you about an inch off the floor (Figure 3–5). Make gentle fists with your hands and place them beside your buttocks, inside of the arm facing front (as in Suzuki statues); or hug yourself

Figure 3–4 Adapted Pilates V

Figure 3–5 Adapted Suzuki Statue

gently to feel the expansion in your back. Deep "huh" sounds are fun to do and/or repeat the sonnet and notice the full, rich quality of your voice! In all of the No Hands, No Feet positions, be sure that your *abdominal action is inward and upward*, so that you are not caving in and squeezing in the chest. Your lower ribs will expand slightly, not contract, as you start to sound.

6. Finally, sit cross-legged and round your torso over your legs; enjoy the sensation that your whole body is breathing. You may want to siren high to low on a hum as you finish this sequence.

The next three exercises are *Destructuring* positions that involve arching your body. They must always be followed by rounding into the Crouch so that your *back is protected* and has ample time to normalize. Low sounds are wonderful in the arches, and in the Bow a huge range of pitches and resonance possibilities can be explored. Allow yourself to produce sounds that are not necessarily pretty, and don't be surprised if you discover an extremely low range that is rather like a voice under the voice. Be sure your throat is wide open but not held rigid. Work with your tongue gently released out of your mouth and your face muscles and eyes thoroughly involved; expect to look ridiculous! Begin vowel sounds with an /h/ to avoid any tendency toward harsh glottal attacks. Think of having an open pipe from the bottom of your torso (or even from your toes) through which the sound releases. Although loudness is possible in these positions, it is not the object of the work, so be gentle and playful and listen to your own body to determine what is appropriate for *you*.

Cobra

The modified yoga Cobra is an advanced version of the Sphinx (see Chapter 1). Lie on your belly and consciously relax your lower body, especially your buttocks and legs. Place the palms of your hands on the floor approximately under your shoulders. Be sure your elbows are touching both the floor and the sides of your torso. *Do not* raise your shoulders nor swing your elbows out like wings at any point. Lift your forehead off the floor to begin the arch; then engage the muscles just underneath your shoulder blades to lift your upper body smoothly. Your arms should straighten but not lock at the elbow, and your shoulders should be down and back throughout (Figure 3–6). If you do not engage the muscles under your shoulder blades, you will struggle to maintain this position, but with those muscles engaged, you should be quite comfortable in the Cobra. Your head and neck should be free.

Check again to be sure you are still released in your lower torso—no clenched buttocks or toes! Use "huh" or "hah" sounds with your tongue out or work on a monologue, one syllable per breath. When you are ready to come out of the arch, take yourself immediately into the Crouch (see Chapter 1) by rounding your body, arms outstretched, knees together or separated, and

Figure 3–6 Modified Cobra

bring your tailbone as close to the ground as possible. Breathe and siren high to low with your tongue out and your lips closed around your tongue. This alternative hum is great for releasing tension in the base of the tongue and should be done with a wide pharynx, as in the initiation of a yawn. You will also find it invaluable when you need to warm up quietly, as in a dormitory or hotel room!

Bow

Lie on your belly and just relax for a moment. Observe your breathing. Don't judge it; just notice it. In the modified yoga Bow, all of the effort is in the legs. *Your arms do not work at all.* Bend your legs and hold your feet with your hands. Let your head hang; do not raise your head. The back of your neck should remain long and released. Now try to straighten your legs; as you do, your body will take on the shape of a bow (Figure 3–7). Stay in the bow shape by *continuously* working in your legs. You

Figure 3–7 Modified Bow

will feel the action of your breath against the floor and will probably be able to access a wide range of vocal noises in this position. The Bow tends to release tension in your neck and
shoulders, and regular practice of this position will strengthen
your legs as well! When you come out of the Bow, go immediately into the Crouch.

Kneeling Arch

On your knees, place the under side of your toes on the
floor (as in being on your toes) and lean forward with your thighs.
Lift your rib cage and circle first one arm, then the other, front to
back, until your hands touch your ankles. Continue to lean
forward with the thighs so that you create an arch and your belly
falls forward, not back (Figure 3–8). The position of your head
should be comfortable; it can be completely released back or
virtually upright. Listen to your own body to determine what is
right for you. This is an excellent position for low "huhs"

Figure 3–8 Kneeling Arch

and "hahs," with or without the tongue out; if your tongue is inside your mouth, be sure it is not bunching up and pulling back away from your lower gum ridge. Or, use spoken text, one syllable per breath, with very strong consonants as a revealing exercise in sound specificity. *Lower abdominal action* should initiate the sound, rather than a downward motion in the upper chest; your *ribs should expand*, not contract, as you begin to speak. When you come out of the exercise, go immediately into the Crouch. If the Kneeling Arch is difficult for you at first, you may modify it by placing a chair behind you and taking your hands to the chair seat instead of to your ankles.

Exploring Resonance

The human voice resonates only in the vocal tract, which includes the larynx, pharynx, mouth and, for some sounds, the nose. Therefore, terms such as *chest resonance, head resonance,* and *mask resonance* describe physical sensations, rather than actual resonating spaces. Likewise, *chest voice* and *head voice* are descriptions of physical sensations. The entire voice resonates in the same space and it is one instrument, not two or more. In the context of this chapter, *resonance* refers to vocal quality rather than to the physical sense of where the sound may *be*.

By now you may have discovered some interesting vocal sounds that you will want to explore further. Feel free to create your own agenda and to work at your own pace. The exercises in this section use specific pitches and may be done on your own or with a group. They are notated for you immediately following the description of each exercise so that you can give yourself pitches from a piano, or other keyboard, or do them without accompaniment if you have absolute pitch.

EXERCISES

Humming

Sit cross-legged on the floor or lie down on your back with your knees up and your feet flat. You should be comfortable, with your spine aligned, shoulders released, back of the neck long, and your jaw letting go. Think of beginning a yawn in the throat as you keep your lips touching gently. Lift your cheeks to make a bit more space in your mouth and be sure your eyes are alive and involved.

1. Start on B-flat below middle C (or down an octave for men) and hum as you move your face a little to be sure it is flexible and not stuck in one position (Figure 3–9a). The

Figure 3–9a Humming

movement is rather like chewing, but work the upper part of your face, not your jaw. Sustain the pitch, using a visual point of focus and/or use your hands to *play* with the sound outside your body; or you may work with a partner. This single sustained pitch is your line. Be sure it is energized to the end and simply release your abs to stop the sound. You may open your mouth slightly to allow breath in; your breathing will be easier and deeper if your lips are separated. Be aware of your breathing. Remember: Abdominal action initiates the sound and your lower ribs move up and out slightly, not in and down, as you begin each line. Move down in pitch by half steps as low as you can sing comfortably. You will need to *relax* into the lowest pitches. Do not push them. The vocal folds vibrate more slowly as you go down in pitch, so focus the tone (keep it clear) and enjoy the sensation of sound in your body.

2. Go up a perfect fifth from your lowest pitch to start the next exercise. For example, if your lowest single pitch is E below middle C, you will begin on B just below middle C and hum down five tones to your low E (Figure 3–9b). Make the movement from one note to another very legato, like syrup, not like a ladder. It may seem messy but that's all right! A critical first step in learning to sing, as in learning to phrase spoken material, is the ability to really connect one note or word to another. That connection is essential to smooth transition from one pitch to another throughout your entire vocal range. Continue the five-note exercise, moving upward by half steps through

Figure 3–9b Humming

F above middle C (downward to B-flat). Be aware of your breathing pattern and continue to move your face gently. Keep space in your throat as if you are closing your mouth on a yawn—don't let your face sag!

Vowel Sequence

1. At F-sharp above middle C, begin to use the vowel *ee* (Figure 3–10a). Work several sequences with your tongue resting gently on your lower lip, cheeks lifted and eyes wide. Yes, you will look really weird but it's worth it! Be sure you are also widening your pharynx and lifting your soft palate so that everything is getting a good stretch.

2. After working up to about C or D above middle C, go back to A or A-flat, now with your tongue inside your mouth and touching (but not pushing against) your lower gum ridge (Figure 3–10b). Keep space in your mouth and continue to lift your cheeks gently as you sing *ee ah ee ah ee*, down the five notes, with *no action* in your jaw! Do not hold the jaw rigid but *isolate the action* of your tongue from that of your jaw. (You can get the sensation of isolating by carrying on a conversation with a partner without using

Figure 3–10a Vowel Sequence

Figure 3–10b Vowel Sequence

your jaw at all.) Be sure your mouth is open about two-fingers width for the *ee* and do not open it further for the *ah*! These two vowels require the greatest possible excursion of the tongue, from highest front vowel to lowest back vowel; the tongue tip should remain behind and touching the lower teeth throughout.

3. When you reach C or D, reverse the order of the vowels, so *ah ee ah ee ah* through F (down to B-flat). Now siren down on an open-throated hum, using your hand(s) at arms length to symbolize and help you focus the tone (Figure 3–10c).

Take the exercise only as high as you can sing with a clear, full-bodied tone. Several concepts may help you to move higher in your range with ease and fullness:

1. Think down and/or move downward physically as you go up in pitch (e.g., move your hand down, point down, or push on the floor or a chair seat as you go higher).

2. Stand and push on a wall as you go higher in pitch or work hand-to-hand with a partner. Pushing will help you engage your abdominals and use the muscles of your chest and back as well.

3. Think of yawning slightly (without retracting your tongue) as you start to sing, so that you maintain space in your throat and keep your larynx comfortably low.

Do a slow siren, high to low, at the end of the exercise using your hand(s) at arm's length to symbolize the sound; be sure your throat remains wide throughout the siren. The siren serves as a mini cool-down after you have worked fairly high in your range.

Figure 3–10c Vowel Sequence

Staccato Arpeggios

In Chapter 1, we worked on all fours and for staccato arpeggios we will again use that position. Feel free to move and/or change positions as you become familiar with the exercise, and continue to think down as you go up in pitch. The arpeggio will be 1, 3, 5, 8, 5, 3, 1 of a major scale, using the *ah* vowel and starting each arpeggio with an /m/. Men should move into falsetto whenever that is comfortable. *Do not* take the exercise higher than you can *sing with ease*. Let it be playful, somewhat like a laugh, and start all but the first tone with a bit of aspiration /h/ so that you avoid a harsh glottal attack. Keep space in your mouth and throat, lift your cheeks, and be sure your tongue stays forward, with the tip resting on the lower gum ridge. All of this lifting and space-making should be done without strain or rigidity, however. It's not about getting into a weird position and muscling to stay there, but rather about freeing yourself of habitual holding that can limit your vocal range, resonance, and expressivity. All of the action of the exercise is in the abdominals and remains abdominal in that it does not discombobulate the rest of your torso. The abdominal action is definite and inward (upward, if you're on all fours) and is followed by an immediate release, so: *in, release, in, release*, and so forth. When you release your belly, your body inhales on its own, quickly and unobtrusively, so that you are doing only one note per breath. No need to chew or reestablish the vowel shape with your mouth; just find that shape and it's there, like the cookie cutter for the sound. You may feel the need for a bit more space in your throat as you go higher in pitch, so your mouth should be flexible, but not working, and your jaw should take a nap!

Practice doing "hah, hah, hah", and so on—deep, low-pitched sounds—several times, as in Chapter 1, just to establish an easy abdominal action before you begin to sing. Then start the exercise about G below middle C and continue as high as you can sing comfortably. For a class, that may be only through a high G or A-flat (top of the arpeggio) at first, but quite soon most

Figure 3–11 Staccato Arpeggios

groups vocalize as high as B-flat or even high C and enjoy it (Figure 3–11). Never push beyond what you can do with your larynx comfortably low. Translated into sensation, do not sing higher than you can go without feeling as if you're reaching for the note, or straining to sing the pitch. On the flip side of that, do not push your larynx down to keep it low! Simply make space (keep the muscle tone or poise) in your throat, enjoy the sensation of singing, and don't worry overly about what your larynx is doing. It is amazingly efficient on its own!

Once you know the exercise well, you may want to move about the room, work with a partner, and/or push on a wall, plié, bow, or curtsey at the top of the arpeggio. Finally, use the siren down several times and be sure you still have your very lowest notes by sustaining a deep "huh" or "hah" while shaking your fists gently or patting yourself on the upper chest and back.

Incorporating Articulation

You have probably used text and/or tongue twisters in some of the exercises already, and I invite you to explore a variety of text, both spoken and sung, in virtually any physical position. At this point, it may be valuable for us to consider what articulates, and what doesn't, in efficient speech. For example, the jaw, which tends to be overly active in much American speech, does not have the primary role it often assumes in the shaping of the vocal tract. Indeed, once you have isolated the activity of your tongue from that of your jaw, you may find that your jaw has been attempting to do the work of your tongue for an infinite number of sounds! The tongue is the great articulator and is more muscular, active, and agile than anything else in the vocal tract. The tongue forms all of the vowel sounds, with the help of the lips for rounded vowels (e.g., *o, oo, aw*), and most of the consonants as it moves about the mouth and throat, interacting primarily with the hard palate, soft palate, and teeth. The lips are critical to the formation of certain consonants (e.g., /m/, /p/, /b/, /w/) and most of the back vowels—formed by the back of the tongue, which lies under the soft palate. Make sure that the activity of your lips is gentle and necessary rather than tense and overdone. With the lips, as well as the tongue, conscious isolation exercises can help to disengage the jaw from any habitual interference with specific sound formations.

Following are several isolation exercises that can be done either singing or speaking in a variety of physical positions. Do them in front of a mirror initially so that you can observe your own habits. In every exercise, the soft palate should be lifted gently and the walls of the pharynx should be wide, as in the initiation of a yawn. Do not overdo these actions, however; you are simply making optimal space in the resonator. The *openness* in your throat will soon begin to feel quite normal, and the ease with which you produce a wide range of pitches and vocal qualities will be a delightful benefit of that space.

EXERCISES

ee ah

First blow through your lips and trill your tongue; make sure that abdominal action starts each trill. Then start to yawn, close your mouth on the yawn, and hum into every part of your face as you move your face energetically. Now starting with your fingertips at your cheekbones, slide your hands downward as you allow them to release your jaw. Don't force your jaw down; just allow it to relax downward and remember that your jaw is not a part of your skull, although it is attached, and that when the jaw relaxes, your mouth is open. So keeping your mouth closed requires muscular effort! Be sure the tip of your tongue is touching your lower gum ridge (not pressing against, just touching) as you say *ee* without lifting your jaw. Your mouth should be open about two-fingers width and your jaw should simply relax and let your tongue work. The front of your tongue (behind the tip and blade) will lift to touch your upper teeth as you produce the *ee* vowel. If you are unsure of what your tongue should be doing or how it should look, roll the tongue out of your mouth, keeping the tip at the lower gum ridge, then bring it back in just enough to say *ee*. Your tongue will be very high on the sides and lifted to your teeth. This is the *ee* position for singing and speaking (Figure 3–12a). In the production of cardinal vowels, which require extreme positions, the lips are tightly spread for *ee*, but spreading the lips to that degree is neither necessary nor desirable for singing and speaking on stage.

Now leaving your jaw in this released, open position, alternate *ee* and *ah* (Figure 3–12b) several times, *smoothly*, with no interruption of the sound. Feel your jaw do nothing as your tongue makes a great motion from one vowel to the other. The tip of your tongue should remain at the lower gum ridge throughout and your throat should feel very open and relaxed, as in the beginning of a yawn. Musical patterns can also be used with *ee ah*.

Figure 3–12a *ee ah*

Figure 3–12b *ee ah*

kah gah

Again, hum as you move your face energetically. Then open your mouth far enough so that you could put two fingers between your front teeth. Keep your jaw relaxed and still and the tip of your tongue touching your lower gum ridge as you say "kah, kah, kah," and so on, and "gah, gah, gah." Make the /k/ and /g/ quite strong as you lift the back of your tongue to your soft palate and release it quickly for the vowel. Watch this action in the mirror to be sure that the tip of your tongue stays forward and that your jaw remains released and uninvolved. Lift your cheeks gently, as in an inner smile, and keep your eyes alive!

Plosives in Rhythm

Almost half the consonants in English are unvoiced; the other half are voiced. To clarify the physical sensation of voicing, place your fingers gently on your larynx as you say /t/, /t/, then /d/, /d/. (Be sure you are not saying "tuh, tuh" and "duh, duh.") With the /t/, you should feel very little activity in your throat; with /d/, however, you will feel vibration as your vocal folds come together to *voice* the sound. In English, there are three pairs of sounds, called *plosives*, that are like little explosions—/p/ and /b/, /t/ and /d/, and /k/ and /g/. Each pair is produced by the same articulatory action; however, one sound is voiceless and the other is voiced. The first two, /p/ and /b/, are bilabial (formed by your two lips), the second, /t/ and /d/, are alveolar (produced by the tip of your tongue against your alveolar ridge), and the third set is velar (produced by the back of your tongue lifting to and releasing from your soft palate).

The following exercise is designed to isolate the articulatory action required for each sound followed by the vowel *ah*, in a rhythm alternating a triplet figure and a long note, as in three (triplet) eighth notes followed by a quarter. Do each of the six parts of the exercise eight times, keeping the sounds very rhythmic and fully connected to the abdominal action you now know. You will probably notice your abdominal muscles moving inward deeply to accent "pah, bah, tah, dah, kah," and "gah," respectively.

- /p/ /p/ /p/ pah, /p/ /p/ /p/ pah, etc., eight times
- /b/ /b/ /b/ bah, /b/ /b/ /b/ bah
- /t/ /t/ /t/ tah, /t/ /t/ /t/ tah
- /d/ /d/ /d/ dah, /d/ /d/ /d/ dah
- /k/ /k/ /k/ kah, /k/ /k/ /k/ kah
- g/ /g/ /g/ gah, /g/ /g/ /g/ gah

Be sure to distinguish clearly between each voiceless plosive and its voiced cognate and use only the action required to produce each sound. For bilabial sounds, the major actors are your lips, not your jaw; for alveolar sounds, the tip of your tongue should do the work with little or no help from your jaw; and for velar sounds, the back of your tongue should be the only actor, with the tip of the tongue remaining relaxed at your lower gum ridge and your jaw staying quiet and uninvolved.

Teeth Together

Put your teeth together, or nearly together (do not grit your teeth), and speak or sing clearly and distinctly without moving your jaw. Do not hold your jaw rigid; rather allow it to relax while your tongue, lips, face muscles, and soft palate do all the work! Be sure to maintain space in your throat so that the sound you produce is full, resonant, and virtually the same as when your mouth is open.

Now, with considerable space in your throat, close your lips and hum as you move your face energetically, leading with your cheeks and eyes. Think of directing the sound into every part of your face and allow your voice to explore a wide range of pitches. High sounds should be especially easy with this movement, but never *push* your voice. Simply allow the sounds to happen and enjoy them!

After experiencing the efficiency of using only the articulator(s) required for clear speech, you may be amazed at how easily you begin to phrase text, both spoken and sung. In Chapter 6, Working with Text, we focus particularly on phrasing techniques and their application in a variety of material.

4 ■ The Voice/Movement Relationship

Apparent Contradictions

Actors frequently experience what seem to be contradictory instructions from one part of their training to another, especially in the areas of voice and movement. Fortunately, practitioners in these fields are beginning to share information and even to integrate work in some instances. However, in many actor training programs, there is little communication and often no crossover information regarding the actor's obvious need to integrate a plethora of physical/vocal training within one coherent, focused, efficient, and available instrument. Breathing is usually at the core of the confusion, and since breathing involves one's entire being, the breathing dilemma and its solution are of necessity a major focus of any integrative approach.

The alignment and breathing required for voice work (see Chapter 1) is quite different from that used in certain dance forms and in some athletic activities as well. Dancers and athletes are seldom concerned with speaking or singing as part of their craft, but actors must be able to use their voices in virtually any physical position, moving or still. Actors play many parts and require a kind of athleticism, grace, and physical skill that is both unconsciously accepted and absolutely expected in professional theatre. Actors may be trained in a variety of movement-related disciplines, including classical dance, modern and jazz, Pilates, yoga, Suzuki, Feldenkrais, stage combat, and the Alexander Technique. Certain of these disciplines teach breathing techniques that seem counter to good voice use in that they restrict movement in the lower ribs and abdomen. Pilates and yoga may also teach a strongly audible inhalation, which causes the vocal folds to work unnecessarily on the in breath and tends to encourage tension in the neck, shoulders, and upper chest. Actors and singers in training are often thoroughly confused by the contradictory sets of directions they receive from movement and dance classes, voice classes, and individual lessons in singing. Moreover, since the matter of contradiction is seldom openly addressed, they are left to sort it out for themselves, usually in an attempt to figure out what is *right*.

What is right in one situation may be quite different from what is right in another. In other words, the body can operate in more than one way. However, when one is primarily an actor and singer, the expansion of the ribs, release of the belly, and silent inhalation are intimate to voice use and to characterization as well. So, are there reasonable compromises one can make? Is it possible to breathe with relative depth, even within the physical restrictions required by some activities? Yes, of course! Many roles require a kind of physicality that is not ideal and with a solid vocal technique the actor still manages to find an *open pipe* to the deep breath necessary for safe and efficient voice use on stage. Movement and dance training can be particularly troublesome and confusing though, if it includes the instruction to restrict the very areas of the body—namely, the lower ribs and abdomen—the performer needs to use in speaking and singing.

Practical Solutions

I'd like to suggest three practical solutions to specific problems that confront the actor and singer who are looking for consistency among physical *truths* in the voice/movement relationship:

1. Communication between movement and voice practitioners

2. Individual adaptation of voice-related breathing patterns to some movement work

3. Use of movement-based exercises in the voice class

When movement and voice are not related and/or integrated for the student, confusion reigns and benefits dissipate. Students hesitate to contradict their teachers, yet teachers seem to contradict one another when the technical differences among respective trainings are not openly acknowledged and discussed. Communication among voice, movement, and dance specialists can go a long way toward helping students make appropriate connections as they access the power and confidence of being both dancer and singer.

Several years ago a gifted young woman came into my graduate class as a well-trained dancer who had done very little voice work. Her vocal quality was shallow and thin and when she needed to be heard in a large space, she went up in pitch and sounded very shrill. During the course of her first year in an MFA acting program, she began to access more low tones, as well as high notes that were open and not pinched. As her breathing became freer and she learned more about the way her voice worked, she also began to eliminate the harsh glottal attacks that had characterized her approach to most vowels. She continued to make remarkable progress throughout the three-year course; in a recent West Coast production of Shakespeare's *A Midsummer Night's Dream*, she *danced* the role of Puck and used her voice with amazing freedom and skill. Her sound was always grounded and full; at the same time, it had the sparkle and agility that were so right for her Puck. Through several years of training and experience she had integrated techniques for voice and movement in such a way that they had become indivisible and totally hers.

Voice and the Triple Threat

The musical theatre professional must be an excellent singer, dancer, and actor and must have the technical skills of those three professions perfectly and unconsciously integrated and available. The Triple Threat is expected to work in widely different musical styles and with directors who may be oblivious to the physical/vocal demands of the material. Therefore, knowing one's own instrument and having the creative and common sense to translate demands into healthful vocal production is critical to the performer's personal health, as well as to the longevity of a career in musical theatre.

Knowing what to do in the event of vocal trouble is essential for any performer and the musical theatre artist is particularly vulnerable to requirements that can lead to vocal strain or injury. A knowledgeable singing teacher can be an invaluable guide throughout a career because as singers and actors, we never outgrow our need for a second, more objective pair of ears and eyes. A word of caution, however. The teacher who is perfect for you at one stage of your career may be different from the teacher who is right for you at another. Also, the teacher who is *fabulous* for your best friend may or may not be good for you. Do not be afraid either to embrace or to reject a teacher and her or his method of training. Over the years you will spend a lot of money on private lessons, which are absolutely essential, so the teachers you choose are critical; consider the following:

1. Beware of the teacher who finds nothing of value in what you are doing. If you have a career, you must be doing something right. You may need to change a lot, but there is obviously a kernel of raw talent and drive that has taken you this far.

2. Be sure your teacher is training singers for the arena in which you want to work and is thoroughly aware of the acting, movement, and dance requirements of musical theatre.

3. Check out your teacher's qualifications, not just as a performer, but also as a professional musician with training in vocal anatomy and physiology, as well as in vocal production.

4. Ideally your teacher relates singing and speaking in a way that allows you to use the same basic technique for both, rather than switching gears, especially in the area of breath management.

5. Your rapport with a teacher has the power to facilitate your learning, so weigh carefully the interactive qualities you experience in the teacher/student relationship.

6. Above all, be exceedingly aware that you, not your teacher, have the primary responsibility for your success. Your teacher can only act as a guide; you must take it from there!

Along with a fine teacher, you will want to have on board an otolaryngologist who specializes in care of the professional voice. Although you may never have a serious vocal problem, you will be very glad to have this specialist as your friend, even when your concerns seem relatively small. Symptoms have a way of appearing at inconvenient moments in a performance schedule, and knowing where to turn immediately can be critical. The Voice Foundation (USA), the British Voice Association, the Canadian Voice Care Foundation, and the Australian Voice Association all maintain lists of doctors throughout the world who specialize in the care and treatment of professional voice users. Contact information for these international organizations can be found in this book's Appendix. Having a video of your vocal folds when they are healthy is also an excellent idea so that the video may then act as a reference in the event of any suspected irregularity.

Over the years, I have questioned seasoned musical theatre actors regarding the breathing challenges of speaking, singing, and dancing on stage. Their answers seem to echo certain common and integrative threads: (1) The actor's breathing adjusts to the nature of the role and most roles don't require the extent of rigidity in the lower torso that may be necessary in pure dance or in a dance class. (2) By the time the actor is working regularly in major productions, the individual technical pieces of voice production and dance have been integrated into a form that is difficult to describe and greater than the sum of its parts.

EXERCISES

The following yoga-based sequence with voice is a particular favorite in classes focusing on singing and makes an exhilarating beginning to a personal workout. The poses are based in Ashtanga yoga and are adapted primarily from the teachings of Rodney Yee (1999), Marika Becz (2001), and Karen Shanley (2000). Allow your breath to do what it will; do not direct it and play with any vocal sounds—loud, soft, high, low, grunts, groans, bits of songs, vocalises. Anything at all that you can produce easily in each position is fine. Remember that high pitches are easy to do in rounded positions and low, even monsterlike sounds, are facilitated by arches. Work frequently with your tongue out resting on your lower lip, with your mouth either open or closed. Maintain space in your throat (Chapter 3) and avoid harsh glottal attacks (Chapter 2).

Stand with your feet together. This is the one sequence in which your feet will not be hip-width apart. Be sure your sternum is high and your tailbone is down but not tucked. Arms by your side. *Allow* your body to breathe rather than directing it, and feel free to use your voice at any time. Don't think about it, just make sounds.

Let your arms float up to shoulder height, palms of your hands facing the floor; bring your hands into a prayer pose, then take them overhead, palms together (Figure 4–1). Feel your shoulder blades going toward your waist (downward) rather than toward your head throughout the sequence. Now, keeping your weight centered, go over into a drop-down; let your torso release from your tailbone so that your back is more flat than rounded. Hang over in whatever way is comfortable for you in this initial stretch (Figure 4–2).

Take your right foot back, then your left foot back into upper push-up (arms extended, toes on the ground). Release your knees to the ground and curve, or swoop, to Upward Dog

Figure 4–1 Hands Overhead

Figure 4–2 Drop-down

Figure 4–3 Upward Dog

(Figure 4–3) without taking your elbows out to the sides like wings; your knees may be touching the ground. Your elbows will always face behind you as in the Cobra. With your tongue out "huh" or "hah" from that deep, underneath place. Go to Downward Dog (Figure 4–4). Your tailbone is high, as in the point of an inverted V; stretch your arms and legs. Repeat twice: knees, Upward Dog, Downward Dog.

Bring your right foot forward into a lunge, arms overhead, palms of your hands together (Figure 4–5). Deep "huhs" or glissando hums with your tongue out are useful choices in this pose. Now go to lower push-up (Figure 4–6), then to Upward Dog (tongue out) and Downward Dog. Repeat, starting with your left foot forward and ending in Downward Dog.

Place your right knee on the ground, turn to the right side, and take your left arm straight up in the air (Figure 4–7). Easy high staccatos are great here. Go to Downward Dog, then repeat on the left side.

Figure 4–4 Downward Dog

Figure 4–5 Lunge

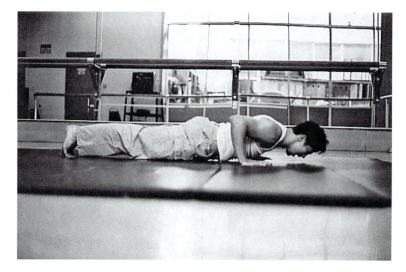

Figure 4–6 Lower Push-Up

Figure 4–7 Side Arm Balance with Knee

Take your right leg into a Cross-Legged Lunge just off the ground; let your weight go forward and engage the muscles under your shoulder blades (Figure 4–8). Struggle sounds may

Figure 4–8 Cross-Legged Lunge

seem perfect in this position! Go to Downward Dog, then repeat on the left side.

Take your feet wide apart, then wrap your right arm around your right ankle or lower calf, first from the inside, then from the outside (Figure 4–9). The stretch is different depending on the

Figure 4–9 Wrap

direction of the wrap. Do this with a flat back; your tailbone will be the highest point of the shape and your head will probably be near your knee. Repeat on the left side, then stretch forward in whatever way you like. Return to Downward Dog.

Take your right foot forward, left foot forward (feet together), and hang over in a drop-down. With the palms of your hands together, come straight up with a flat back—not too fast— and take your arms overhead. Keep your weight centered and think of your shoulder blades moving down toward your waist as your arms move up.

Now let your arms float down to your sides, as in the beginning of the sequence. Then float them up to shoulder height and take your whole torso straight over into Airplane Pose (Figure 4–10). Your neck is long, your head is in line with your spine, and you are facing the floor. Lip and tongue trills may seem appropriate here, and feel free to fly the plane a bit if you're so inclined! Your back will be flat; your arms are out to the side.

Figure 4–10 Airplane Pose

Now let your arms release as you go into a drop-down and observe any changes in your body and breath since the beginning of the sequence. Take your left foot back, then your right foot back into lower push-up, Upward Dog, and Downward Dog.

Balancing on your right arm, take your body to the right side and keep your legs straight. Take your left arm straight up in the air and maintain the length and width of your body (Figure 4–11). High staccato passages are wonderful in this position! Follow with Downward Dog and repeat on the other side. In Downward Dog remember to keep your tailbone high and get a good stretch in your arms and legs. Do not overstretch, however; simply listen to your body and work accordingly. Sirens high to low, as well as other sounds throughout your range are easy in Downward Dog. They also provide opportunities for you to integrate vocal qualities so that you move easily from one part of your range to another.

Now come to sitting and bring one knee in to your chest. Keep your sternum high, shoulders low, and neck long. Use your

Figure 4–11 Side Arm Balance

voice, and notice that the automatic (inward/upward) action of your lower abdominals triggers an opening, or outward, movement in your lower ribs. Release that leg and repeat on the other side. Extend both legs and shake them out gently.

Sit with your legs outstretched, arms by your side. Place your hands on the floor and thrust your chest forward and up. Do not lean back; this is a gentle arch so there is little or no weight on your arms. Low pitches are easy here. Now engage the muscles under your shoulder blades and lift your body into a slant or wedge shape, adjusting your feet as necessary (Figure 4–12). Your buttocks will be in line with the rest of your body rather than dropping down, and your shoulders will be low so that your neck is long. Let your head be wherever it is comfortable. This is a favorite position for text work. Try using one syllable per breath, as in a gentle, simple staccato. Your belly will go down toward the floor to initiate each sound and will release upward for the in breath. Do not expect your voice to sound

Figure 4–12 Wedge Shape

normal; it may go to a deep, even growly place. Be sure to form and release your consonants fully and maintain space in your throat regardless of the position of your head. As a useful image, think of having space *behind* your soft palate.

Come out of the position slowly. Lengthen the back of your neck and round your head forward as you bring your knees toward the center of your body. You may want to lace your fingers together, place them on your head, and allow the weight of your arms to stretch your neck very gently. Remember that you may always use your voice and that whimpers, sighs, and other unconventional sounds are just as valid as speaking or singing. At the same time, do not feel obligated to use voice. Simply enjoy the physicality of what you are doing and give your voice permission to do what it will.

Now let your knees fall outward and put the soles of your feet together; bring your feet inward toward your torso. Be sure your sternum is high, spine aligned, shoulders released down, and the back of your neck long.

1. Using your hands or forearms, press down gently on your legs as they resist. You are working your inner thighs. Do a few open-sounding, low-pitched "huhs" and/or a bit of text. Think of having an open pipe, or even a straw, that goes all the way down to the bottom of your torso and allows your breath to do the same.

2. Now relax your legs and press them down gently with your hands or forearms, or hold your ankles with your hands and slide your elbows slowly outward toward your knees, to stretch your inner thighs and encourage greater flexibility at the leg/torso connection (Figure 4–13). Repeat at least once.

Lie down on your back and bring one leg straight up in the air. Grab your big toe, if possible, or your ankle or calf, to give that leg one final stretch (Figure 4–14). Your resting leg may remain flat or you may bend your knee. If you raise your head, keeping the

Figure 4–13 Inner Thigh Stretch

Figure 4–14 Leg Stretch

back of your neck long, the pitch of your voice will tend to go up; so explore, but never push, allow but don't plan. As you lower your leg, consciously use your pelvic floor muscles (in the groin) to maintain the balance and stability of your lower torso, and don't hold your breath! Repeat with the other leg, then lie with your arms outstretched, palms of your hands facing the ceiling, and your legs released. Notice your breath, make sounds if you like, and briefly recall your journey through the sequence.

This is an easy set of exercises that almost anyone can do. Feel free to modify them, however, to your own particular requirements. If you are not already into Ashtanga yoga, this may take you there, and as you learn even more challenging poses, I encourage you to do them with sound and without predetermining your breathing pattern. If you are in a yoga class, of course, you will probably go with the instructions given, but on your own you are free to make adaptations that can strengthen you vocally, as well as physically.

References

Becz, M. 2001. Classes in Voice and Movement, California State University, Fullerton.

Yee, R. 1999. *Power Yoga for Beginners: Strength.* Santa Monica: Living Arts Video.

Shanley, K., 2000. Pilates Classes, Anaheim Ballet, Anaheim.

Suggested Reading

Gelb, M. H. 1994. *Body Learning.* New York: Holt.

McEvenue, K. 2001. *The Alexander Technique for Actors.* London: Methuen Drama.

Melton, J. 2001. "Pilates Training and the Actor/Singer." *Australian Voice,* 7: 13–15. Brisbane: Australian National Association of Teachers of Singing.

PART II

Performance Details

5 ■ Reading Music

Overview

Many actors auditioning with sixteen bars of a song have no idea what the squiggles on the page mean when they see a piece of music. Not knowing a language in written form can put you at a distinct disadvantage. Whenever I work with actors on singing, I insist that they learn to read music, at least minimally, for their own efficient and accurate work on material, and for their literate communication with accompanists and music directors.

People frequently have the idea that reading music is the ability to see a note on a page and sing it immediately, without help from a piano or other instrument. That ability, commonly referred to as having absolute pitch, or pitch recognition, is usually discovered rather than developed and is not directly connected with music notation. Reading music is, rather, the ability to understand relationships in a language that involves sounds and silences that occur in *time*. Music expresses itself and has its own forms, in addition to being a vehicle for the expression of other languages (e.g., English, French, Spanish) and their literal and contextual meanings. When you sing, you give priority to the *spoken* language in that your breathing and phrasing are based on what you are doing as an actor and the word language through which you are doing it. A thorough understanding of the musical language underlying and supporting your words, however, can add richness and detail to your work

Learning to read music can be fascinating and can open up options undreamed of by the rote learner who habitually copies *originals* instead of *being* an original! Whatever the song or aria, think of it as having been written for you. No one else has done it. You must find your own definitive way with it and in the final analysis, *your way* comes out of your work as an actor. What happens to your voice in the process will be right if your technique is solid and you *act*.

There are many books and courses designed to teach you to read music quickly and efficiently. Choose a training approach that focuses on your particular needs. If you are a classical singer, music reading is probably a given in your life and you are or have been in a music degree program. If you are an actor or musical theatre specialist, however, your needs may be somewhat different. The remaining sections of this chapter focus specifically on those needs. Whatever your career goals, music reading will mean understanding *physically*, as well as intellectually, the relationships of rhythm, tempo, sound, and color in the context of communicating the *play* to the audience. Knowing the idiosyncrasies of particular styles of music is also invaluable and will enable you to sing in more than one way with confidence and accuracy.

When you are studying singing, you may do well to learn and to perform classical material along with songs from musical theatre and other nonclassical genres. Both classical and musical theatre trainings usually include a healthy respect for the notes on the page. It is possible to sing any kind of music without being able to read it, of course; but, understanding music notation and taking it off the page for yourself, is both exciting and necessary if you are not simply to mimic other performers.

Specific Requirements for the Actor

If you are working in musical theatre, you will need to have considerable skill as a musician and playing the piano at least minimally is a necessity. Even if you do not consider yourself a musical theatre actor, being able to pick out your vocal line on the piano or other keyboard instrument will allow you to teach yourself new music quickly—as at an audition or callback! So use the piano as a visual aid and work with it whenever possible as you explore new material.

Reading music accurately involves much more than knowing the right pitch. *Rhythm* gives music its shape; without rhythm, pitches are just blobs of sound, like clay that has yet to be worked. You will need to understand the rhythmic patterns that are integral to what the composer has written so that you can execute those patterns accurately and not just *sort of*. Some styles will even require *bending* the rhythm, as in singing a dotted eighth note followed by a sixteenth as the first and third parts of a triplet; however, such peculiarities will be learned as performance practices once you have the basic skills required to read music as it is notated. The notation system for music is not perfect in that it cannot communicate fully all that you do as an artist when you perform; however, knowing what is there enables you to come from a place of integrity, and to give the same respect to the composer and librettist as to the playwright.

A part of reading music for the singer is understanding how the words *fit*, or don't fit the musical phrases. Also, the words to songs often rhyme. The study of poetic text is invaluable for the actor and provides much of the technical information required for the performance of songs as well. In general, do not be a slave to the musical phrase or to the regularity that may seem implied by a lyric that rhymes. Working on song texts as spoken pieces, especially before you sing them, and going for what you want as an actor instead of singing the words mindlessly, is essential to reading the music correctly. When you are dealing with good material, the lack of fit between music and words can be delightful and far more interesting than an endless series of matching phrases. However, in material that is not brilliant, words that don't fit the music can simply be awkward and challenging. If you have accepted the role, you've accepted the challenge! However, if you don't need to do the piece, choose something else—something that works *for* you instead of against you; and if you need help choosing material, keep asking for suggestions and *reading* new songs until you find several that you love and can do well, especially for auditions.

Guidelines for Preparing Material

In addition to choosing music and preparing songs for auditions, you have the added responsibility of getting the written music ready to be used by an accompanist. Once again, this requires your ability to read and understand the music you have chosen. If the key of the written music is not comfortable for you, you *must* have it transposed before you use it in an audition, otherwise you are asking for trouble! Indeed, you must do everything you can to make the written form of the music accompanist friendly. For example, you need to indicate in large, bold writing any cuts you are making, where you will start and stop, whether you will need an introduction (if so, what it should be), and any interpolations and/or unexpected changes of tempo you have planned. If you can bring your own accompanist to the audition, of course, that is ideal; but most actors do a lot of auditioning and work with many different accompanists in the process. Be sure you have worked on your songs thoroughly with an accompanist before you use them and that you can find your first pitch easily from the introduction or single pitch (often called a bell tone) the accompanist will play.

Most auditions require 16 bars of a song or sometimes as few as 8 bars. This does not necessarily mean that you will do exactly 16 or 8 bars. You will do a logical section of the piece, which may be 14 bars or 17, or another number near but not exactly 16. Likewise, with 8 bars. The beginning of the song is seldom the place to find an appropriate 16 bars. Instead, go to the end of the song and work backward to see if there is a logical last section that you can do. Sometimes starting at the bridge, or middle section, of the piece and going to the end is possible. In addition, you may need to exchange one set of lyrics for another in order to say what you want to say. Cutting a song is similar to cutting a spoken monologue for audition purposes. Ask for advice from your teacher and/or your regular accompanist and be sure to rehearse the piece in each version you decide to use. The section(s) you perform should show off your strengths and let the auditors know very quickly that you can do whatever is required for the part you want. If you are singing an up-tempo song, you may be able to do 32 bars (or 16 in the shorter version). Again, see if there is a good section at the end of the piece, then explore other possibilities if that doesn't work. The end of the song is often best because it has a good finish and if you can nail the *money note* you will end brilliantly!

As you prepare the written music, it is good to know what is preferred—a binder with music in protective covers (nonglare, please!), music in a binder without protective covers (so there is no problem at all with glare from plastic), or music on stiff sheets of paper taped together so that they lay out as one piece onto the piano. The third option is probably the least likely and would never be used for more than three sheets. The binder seems to be the the way to go. Certainly don't take in a collection of music with your song somewhere in the middle. Don't ever take in individual photocopied sheets! Don't *ever* take in a lead sheet (your line of music only with chord symbols and no written accompaniment). Don't ever take in a song in the wrong key with chord symbols for the key you want written in. Don't ever take in a song in the wrong key and ask the accompanist to transpose it on sight! And when you put music in a binder, be sure it is back to back, as in a book. In addition, put in your binder *only* what you are prepared to sing *now.* You may be asked to sing anything in the binder. Therefore, if you are prepared to do the entire song from which you have chosen 16 bars, have the entire song available; if you are not, don't have it in the binder! You might want to have at least three versions of the same song in your binder, clearly marked: the whole song, a 16-bar cut, an 8-bar cut.

Always know what key you are singing in and know the note you start on. Ideally, be able to go to the piano and play a little of your song by ear. You do not have just one key in which you'll always sing; you will sing different songs in different keys. You do have a vocal range that is comfortable for you to use in a song. You may vocalize several notes higher and lower than that range, but it is seldom wise to sing your absolute extreme limits because your voice will sound richer and more comfortable if you have something in reserve. Ask your teacher to help you define your range for purposes of a résumé and in answer to questions regarding your highest and lowest notes.

Get several good audition songs that you can use again and again. You should have at least:

1. A ballad, or slow song that is sustained and shows off your voice
2. An up-tempo, or faster song
3. One or more *acting* pieces, or songs that show your strengths as an actor
4. A character song
5. A specialty song that shows some particular aspect of your talent, expertise, and/or interest (e.g., country, pop, jazz, or rock)

The greater the variety the better. Also, look at music from more than one era; for example, include a classic musical theatre song from Rodgers and Hart, Rodgers and Hammerstein, Cole Porter, or Gershwin along with songs from musicals that have been written more recently. Regardless of your choices, be sure that everything you have is dynamite for you. It is far better to have less in your binder and do it well than to have a lot of material that does not really show you off.

One particular word of caution regarding material. There is always a list of songs *not* to do, and the songs on that list are often your very favorite songs! The list changes frequently, so check with your teacher or accompanist for the latest information. It is always possible, of course, to do a song so well that you can break the rules; however, in most circumstances, it is good to avoid the songs on that list. Also avoid songs that are difficult for the accompanist to read. The simpler and more straightforward your accompaniment the better your chance of having a positive experience with the song.

Read the specifications carefully when you are preparing for auditions. The songs you have in your binder, or *book*, should represent a range of characters that you might play, as well as a range of musical styles. Choose material with that in mind and do the best you can to match what you have with what is required in each situation. Occasionally, you will need to learn something new in a hurry, either because it is especially important and you want to sing exactly the right thing, or because you are auditioning for a new show and the material has not been available in advance.

Working with an Accompanist

The accompanist can make or break your audition, and your interaction with the accompanist is critical to your success. You will work with wonderful accompanists, mediocre accompanists, and accompanists that are really bad. No matter. When it is an audition situation, you must be gracious, do the best you can, and never blame the accompanist openly or otherwise for anything that goes wrong. Accompanists play for a zillion auditions in a day so you are just one of many singers who want to be cast. The accompanist would like you to be good. It's a lot more fun to play for someone who is good than someone who is ill-prepared and not very interesting. Chances are no one will know better than the accompanist how accurate you were, how good a musician you are, and how well you ensemble with another person. In addition, the accompanist probably has the ear of the people who are casting the show. You get the picture!

When you walk into an audition, take your music to the accompanist, say "hello" but don't start up a conversation. Put your music on the piano or give it to the accompanist, let him or her know what you're doing (it is clearly marked, of course), whether you want an intro or a bell tone, and what your tempo will be. Also, is there a physical or vocal cue for the intro? It is fine to glance at the accompanist as a cue; or if you are going into the song immediately following a spoken monologue, you may want to use a line or movement instead. Whatever the cue, do *not* look at the accompanist during the song (there are exceptions, of course, when the accompanist gets in on the act) and do not follow the accompanist. You are *the star, you* are the leader of the ensemble, not the accompanist, so play that role with confidence and style! When your audition is over, go to the accompanist to collect your music and *thank* the accompanist. Don't discuss what went right or wrong, just get your music, say "thank you," and move quickly out of the space.

The major technical difference in auditioning with a song is that you don't do it alone, so regular work with your own accompanist is a must. Even if you can't afford a lot of time, a few sessions with a good and knowledgeable person are absolutely essential. You may learn a song on your own and think you're ready to perform it, but singing it with an accompanist is different and you need time to adjust to that dynamic. An accompanist can be a valuable friend who gives you honest feedback about your work. She or he may also be able to help you with the selection and preparation of material, as well as with transpositions and arrangements that are right for you.

Guidelines for Performance

All of the same techniques and qualities you use as an actor apply when you are singing. You may change the use of your voice from one role to another, from one dialect to another, and even from one scene or part of a scene to another, but the core of what you are doing is *acting*. The fact that what you are saying in the scene is so charged with emotion and/or significance that you sing it, is powerful information in itself.

We often load singing with expectations and judgments that actually prevent us from singing well. Auditors and audiences respond positively to a total package, not just to a pretty sound. So, develop a solid vocal technique, learn your music accurately, know the style of the material you have chosen, rehearse thoroughly with your accompanist, then release all that, knowing that it will be there for you when you are not thinking about it.

Recommended Reading

Robison, K. 2000. *The Actor Sings*. Portsmouth: Heinemann.

6 ■ Working with Text

Overview

Although we may never understand completely all that is happening, physiologically and psychologically, as we perform, valuable clues from voice science, performance experience, and the body's own intuitive actions enable us to refine what we do to get what we want. This chapter takes care of the nitty-gritty speech details that often get in the way of your doing the rest of the work easily, and it provides specific suggestions for working on phrasing, especially with texts that are sung. Many of the techniques used with spoken text also can be applied to texts that are sung. In the event that you have not encountered the great master teachers of spoken text, I invite you to read, in particular, the books of Cicely Berry (1973, 1992, 2001), Patsy Rodenburg (1992, 1993, 1998, 2002), and Kristen Linklater (1976, 1992).

As you work with text, you may need to acknowledge your own regional speech habits and their value, especially when they are appropriate to the material. At the same time, you must be able to move from one set of habits to another, as in accents and dialects that are far removed from your habitual speech. You will need to understand physiologically, as well aurally, the specifics of: (1) your own regional dialect; (2) the *neutral*, or standard of the country(s) in which you are working; and (3) the changes in resonance and articulation that are required to move you from one set of habits to another. Regardless of the dialect, clarity of communication through the language is critical to performance, in sung as well as spoken material.

Working with text, as it relates to vocal technique, involves conscious work on the use of breath in phrases of various lengths so that your breathing is efficient and easy regardless of the material. Breathing problems are seldom the result of not having *enough* breath, but rather of not using the breath efficiently. Trying to *fill up* the lungs by sucking the breath in is a common method of doing ourselves in. Not managing the breath efficiently as we speak or sing is another way we put ourselves at a disadvantage. By now, you should have some basic technical skills that you can trust and your work with text can take you to the level of performance.

Elements: Vowels and Consonants

Any *extreme* use of the voice can distort words and the communication of meaning through words. Therefore, vocal sounds that are at the extremes of your pitch range, volume range, and/or pace range (fast/slow) will require an extra measure of articulatory energy in performance. Singing also distorts words in that it lengthens vowels past their normal speech value and inherently tempts the singer to glorify the vowels at the expense of the consonants. Thus, we frequently hear this sort of comment: "The opera was in English but I'm glad there were subtitles because I couldn't understand it." I am aware that there are vocal and musical values that may outweigh the need for the words to be understood in some instances, but when what we experience as the audience is glorious sound emanating from singers who appear to be going through some sort of intense emotional response, we are relegated to the rank of observer and never privileged to participate. The drama is confined to the stage and does not touch us, so the play is not communicated to the audience. We may feel great excitement about the beauty and technical prowess of the voices, but how much more we might experience if the singers actually dealt with the language and gave it to us in understandable form.

Consonants are to vowels what rhythm is to pitches. Consonants provide shape and contour to the language. We learn to produce pure vowels and clearly formed diphthongs when speaking and singing; we learn to move smoothly from one vowel to another without interrupting the vocal line; and we work text without the consonants so that the language will flow. This kind of training is essential for the actor and singer. By the same token, we must give careful attention to the clear, crisp, accurate, sensuous production of consonants so that when we put the two together we have an appropriate balance. The following are exercises that separate the elements, then reconnect them. You can use the exercises with virtually any text, (e.g., a song from musical theatre, a Shakespeare sonnet, or an operatic aria).

EXERCISES

Vowels Only

Speak or sing several lines of your text using *only* the vowels. Be very specific about exactly which vowel, diphthong, or triphthong you are doing and *do not make any breaks* between vowels! Let your voice flow smoothly in an absolutely legato line from one vowel to the next, and phrase the text as you would speak it. If you are not sure how to do this, sing "Happy Birthday" to a friend using only the vowels. Ah hah! You must think the text, so this is not just a mental exercise in which you pick out the vowels and say them.

Remember to pronounce the vowel in "the" as *ee* before another vowel sound and *uh* (schwa) before a consonant sound—so "th*ee* apple," "th*ee* orange" and "th*uh* dress," "th*uh* shirt." Note also that it will be "th*ee* hour," "th*ee* honorable," and so on, because there is no consonant sound at the beginning of those words.

Before we move on to consonants, here are a few clarifications regarding vowels, diphthongs, and triphthongs. A vowel or vowel combination makes up the core of most syllables in English and in many other languages as well. Some words, however, use a sustainable consonant, often called a syllabic consonant, instead of a vowel in one or more syllables—for example, in the second syllable of the contractions *didn't, couldn't, wouldn't, shouldn't*; in the first syllable of words such as *constituency* and *completely*; and in the second syllable of *little* and *bottle*. In Standard American and British RP, only three consonants are used syllabically: /l/, /m/, and /n/.

A single, or pure, vowel is made with one shape in the vocal tract (e.g., *ah* and *ee*), and if you change that shape even slightly, you change the vowel. A diphthong (pronounced *difthong*) is a two-vowel combination that serves as one sound in a single syllable of text (e.g., *a* as in *day* and *o* as in *blow*). Your tongue changes positions from one vowel to the next as it forms the diphthong. A triphthong (*trifthong*) is a three-vowel combination that serves as the vowel element in a single syllable, as in the words *fire, tire,* and *our, shower*. If you do the words in slow motion, you will feel and hear the individual vowels. When you are singing, sustain only the first vowel and form the other one or two quickly as you complete the syllable. However, if you are working in a dialect that distributes vowel weights differently, you may need to elongate the second or third vowel as well.

If you have studied phonetics, this is all very elementary, and if you have not studied phonetics, I strongly urge you to do so! Knowing the phonetic alphabet will enable you to represent virtually every possible speech sound in written form. It will also make you infinitely easier to work with in production situations, and for accents and dialects it is a must!

As you are doing the vowel exercise, note that in Standard American and Standard British /r/ is fully produced *only* when it precedes a vowel. In Standard British there will be no sound of /r/ before a consonant and in Standard American there will be /r/ *coloring* but not a strong and fully formed /r/. Therefore, in words like *heart* and *performance,* the /r/ is silent in British speech and a coloration, or movement of the tongue toward, but not to an /r/ in American speech. In many American dialects, of course, the /r/ is full and fairly strong regardless of where it is in the word. Look carefully at a word like *mirror* though to see what is vowel and what is consonant and what sounds actually belong to each syllable. In English, double consonants mean little or nothing in terms of pronunciation, so there is one /r/ sound in the middle of the word and either no /r/ or /r/ coloring at the end. The first syllable contains an initial consonant, /m/, plus the vowel *ih.* The second syllable begins with /r/, is followed by the *schwa,* or short neutral vowel, and in American speech may conclude with /r/ coloring. So the first syllable is *mih,* not *mihr.* In singing especially, an elongated /r/ tends to block the resonating space in the mouth and distort the word. American speakers generally produce an /r/ by pulling the tongue back and bunching it up so that both the tongue and jaw are tense. It's rather like putting a mute in a horn. Actors, however, must learn to produce the /r/ with the tip of the tongue lifting toward but not to the hard palate so that medial /r/ sounds become cleaner and surrounding vowels are freed from an otherwise inordinate amount of /r/ coloring.

Whatever your text, know the appropriate dialect for the material and be sure that is what you are going for. If you are doing a musical or opera that requires both singing and speaking, keep the dialect consistent from one use of your voice to the other. The major adjustments that singers often make going from speaking to singing have to do with keeping the vowels *pure,* because the voice operates more efficiently and sounds better when the vowels are true and specific. That same specificity should apply to speaking as well and can help the singer maintain a consistency between lines that are sung and lines that are spoken.

Consonants Only

Now take the same text used for the Vowels Only exercise and speak the consonants without the vowels. Again, you must think the text, and this time you will not be able to be legato. With stopped plosives, contextual execution is usually impossible, of course, since a preceding vowel is required to effect the stopped sound. Therefore, you will probably aspirate all /p/, /t/, and /k/ sounds and fully produce /b/, /d/, and /g/ sounds in the exercise. The final /t/ of *that* in the combination *that time* is an example of a stopped plosive. In English, we often stop plosives when they precede other consonants so that we can connect smoothly from one sound to the next. The sound is stopped by placing the appropriate articulators in the position of the consonant and leaving them there rather than completing the consonant action and releasing the breath (e.g., as in the second /p/ of *popcorn*). There are frequent exceptions to the use of stopped sounds, especially in singing, because of the distortion factor. This is true also in any text that demands a stronger production of the sound than stopping would provide (e.g., in a highly emotional scene when you are working at vocal extremes).

Please note that nasals are hums and can be sustained, so the bilabial nasal /m/ is *mmmm*, not *muh*. Likewise the alveolar nasal /n/ is *nnnnn* instead of *nuh*—even when it is at the end of a phrase in a song! The velar nasal, spelled *ng*, is neither an /n/ nor a /g/, but a hum produced by lifting the back of the tongue to the soft palate while the tip of your tongue remains *down* at the lower gum ridge. In American speech, and especially on the West Coast, /n/ is frequently substituted for *ng* in all words ending in *ing* so that we hear *een* instead of *ihng* in words like *singing, speaking, laughing*, and *crying*. Be sure the tip of your tongue stays down and let the back of your tongue do the work for *ng*.

Reconnect

Now speak or sing the text using all of the speech sounds and observe how rich and full it is. Notice how the sounds themselves help you to express the meaning and intent of the words. Fully producing the words will prevent you from making everything alike because the sounds themselves are not alike. Some vowels tend to be long (extended), others are short; some consonants are voiced, others are unvoiced; and some consonants can last as long as your breath, while others are very quick. Take the time that is required to produce each sound and never feel you must rush to the next word or syllable. Sounds that are produced quickly will go by quickly and those that need more time will have it. Your speech rhythms will become far more interesting and your kinesthetic experience of the language will be heightened. Suddenly, your articulatory activity will be pleasurable; the freedom to speak the words completely will assist your communication of their meaning; the dual dimensions of sound and sense will be experienced by your audience; and your physical commitment to the language will have a freeing effect on your voice.

Phrasing and Connected Speech, Spoken and Sung

We speak and sing phrases of many different lengths, from a single word or a sigh to several lines of text on a single breath. We need to know that we have the technique to do that without a struggle and without focusing on it in performance. So we go to the vocal gymnasium, daily! Speaking and singing on stage is unnatural, in that it requires far more athletic prowess than everyday conversation. Not only do we need to know the notes and the rhythms and the words, and who we are, where we've been, why we're here, and what we want, but we may regularly play eight shows a week in all kinds of venues for hundreds of people who want us to be fabulous every time. So, we have to know what we're doing, especially with the breath. The following exercises focus on building strength, flexibility, and capacity, as well as a feeling of ease in those areas of the body most directly concerned with breath management.

Exercises

Side Stretches

This exercise is adapted from Pilates training and works on flexibility and expansion in the rib cage. It involves twisting the torso, so read the instructions carefully, work gently, and do the exercise only if it seems right for you. The twist itself I call a *handicap* position because it forces you to find your way through the twist to a released belly and abdominal muscles that are free to work. Once again, the image of an open pipe or a straw may be useful.

Sit cross-legged on the floor and think of lifting the pelvic floor so that your energy is going up. Check to be sure that your sternum is high, back of the neck long, shoulders released down, and your spine in neutral (neither rounded forward nor arched back). Let your left hand, or fingertips, touch the floor as far to the left side as comfortable. Lift your right arm to the side, palm of the hand facing up, and think of reaching as you move the arm through imaginary resistance. As you lift your arm, think of your right shoulder blade going down, or contrary to the direction of your arm, so that you do not lift the shoulder as well. Take the right arm toward your left side directly over your head and feel the stretch in your rib cage on the right side (Figure 6–1). Put little or no weight on your left arm. Use your voice at any time, or just breathe and be aware of any differences in your breathing from one part of the exercise to another. Slowly return to your starting position and repeat twice.

On the second repetition, do not return immediately to the starting position. Instead, turn your whole torso to the left so that both hands, or perhaps only your fingertips, are on the floor (Figure 6–2). Keep your torso erect and use your voice. You may want to start with a "huh." Make sure that you release your belly and find your low sounds first. Think of keeping the pipe as open as possible, in spite of the twist. Now unwind slowly, move your torso a bit so that it feels comfortable and repeat the sequence on the other side.

Figure 6–1 Side Stretch

Figure 6–2 Twist

The Counting Exercise

This is a Fitzmaurice-based exercise designed to teach breath management for phrases of various lengths. It may be done in virtually any position, moving or still, but the classic way of learning it is lying on your back with your knees up, feet flat on the floor, and your spine in neutral. Or you may choose to: (1) sit cross-legged on the floor; or (2) stand facing a wall and lean (don't push) against the wall, keeping the back of your neck long and your shoulders released down. If you are lying or sitting, you will be able to monitor the actions of your intercostal and abdominal muscles by placing one hand on your lower ribs, at the side, and the other on your belly as low as possible.

Count to 9 or 10 and back in a steady rhythm using the word *by* in between the numbers. The inhalation for each phrase will occur automatically as you release your abdominal muscles on a silent count. Once you have done the exercise a couple of times, you will focus more specifically on the ribs, but initially, just be sure that you are letting go and not holding your belly tight on the silent beat. If you are in a class, you might have someone accompany the exercise on a drum or other percussion instrument.

1 (*beat*)
1 by 2 (*beat*)
1 by 2 by 3 (*beat*)
1 by 2 by 3 by 4 (*etc.*)
1 by 2 by 3 by 4 by 5
1 by 2 by 3 by 4 by 5 by 6
1 by 2 by 3 by 4 by 5 by 6 by 7
1 by 2 by 3 by 4 by 5 by 6 by 7 by 8
1 by 2 by 3 by 4 by 5 by 6 by 7 by 8 by 9
1 by 2 by 3 by 4 by 5 by 6 by 7 by 8
1 by 2 by 3 by 4 by 5 by 6 by 7
1 by 2 by 3 by 4 by 5 by 6
1 by 2 by 3 by 4 by 5
1 by 2 by 3 by 4
1 by 2 by 3
1 by 2
1

Now focus primarily on the ribs as you repeat the exercise and take the numbers higher than ten if you like. On the silent beat, your ribs will expand (and your abdominals will release), and you will note the need for more expansion as the numbers get higher. The greatest expansion will be lateral and posterior (sides and back) in the lower ribs, and you should be able to monitor that expansion with your hands. Your ribs will float down slowly as you use breath but they should never feel squeezed. In other words, you don't want the *sponge* to be compressed to smaller than its neutral size (see Chapter 2). It is a good idea, however, to know the feeling of going too long on a single breath so that you can avoid that kind of breath use on stage. Speak anything and continue to speak until you feel you are being squeezed in the chest and are working on the *end* of your breath. This is poor breath management and you'll usually feel out of control if you overextend in this manner. Now speak or sing the text again, be aware of where you are in your phrasing and allow yourself to breathe before you get to the point of squeezing.

This exercise leads naturally into working with other texts. So take a piece that you are singing or speaking and continue to monitor the ribs as you do it. Note that as you begin each phrase, the deep action of your abdominal and pelvic floor muscles causes a further expansion at bottom of the rib cage. You can monitor this action with your fingertips in the cutaway, or soft area between your lower ribs in front, as well as at the sides and back of your chest.

Now take your direct attention away from the physical actions of breath management and speak or sing any phrases you like, as you maintain a feeling of openness in the chest and freedom in your pelvis. Feel free to move, especially in a fluid manner that may be dancelike or otherwise. Note any observations orally or in a notebook.

Finally, some critical points regarding: (1) fitting the words together in connected speech, and (2) maintaining good phonatory habits on stage and off. In connected speech we do far more than simply string together a series of perfectly pronounced words. Spoken languages and their respective dialects have individual and specific ways of communicating; tune and rhythm are perhaps the most obvious elements in that individuality. English, regardless of the dialect, is a stress-based language in that some syllables are accented and others are not; therefore stress can be as important to communication as pronunciation. In singing, English is often flattened out so that the natural stresses of words and syllables are lost and what is communicated is sound without sense. How many times have we gone to a concert, opera, or performance of nonclassical music and enjoyed the sounds, emotional connections, forms, structures, rhythms, humor, and technical skill of the performers without understanding many of the words, ideas, or subtle details that were intended to be part of the performance? It was a wonderful event, but we missed a lot of it.

Communicating the sung language as it is spoken can make a world of difference for you, the performer, as well as for the audience. When you sing the language as you would speak it, you have to commit to what you're saying. When you just make pretty sounds, the words could be nonsense; it is easy to focus on your own voice and vocal technique and you are protected from actually interacting with other singers and/or with the audience. Learning to sing as you would speak is a wonderful adventure and necessitates both knowing the language well (English or any other) and being willing to make less of some sounds if the language is stress-based. For example, if the syllable contains a schwa, or the quick, throwaway neutral vowel, as in the indefinite article written *a*—*a* dress, *a* shirt, *a* table—don't blow up that tiny connecting word so that it sounds like more than it is. Even when unstressed syllables have some length musically, they must be given less weight vocally than if they were stressed.

Sung Conversations

Carry on a conversation with a partner about anything (e.g., what mode of transportation you used to get to class, what you had for breakfast, your favorite sport, what you're doing on the weekend) and *sing* the conversation. Don't be concerned with a tune or a style, just allow your voice to sing without thinking about it—and don't mind being over the top! What you *must* think about is what you are saying to your partner. And you must *listen* to your partner so that whatever you say is a response to what you have *heard*. Remember: The most important person on the stage is your partner (not you!), and the actor who really listens is fascinating to watch. Even when you are on stage alone, as in a recital, you must be listening not to the sound of your own voice but to the responses of your partner, real or imagined, and you must have a reason to say what you are saying.

Feel free to do this exercise in any physical position, e.g., sitting cross-legged on the floor facing each other, standing or moving about.

Line Endings

The most important word is often at the end of the line and your breath energy must be there for that word and beyond. Exercises in breath management can get you there technically but your attention and commitment to what you are saying also must be present. Many actors have a tendency to *drop off* the ends of lines: the pitch of the voice drops, volume decreases, and the final sounds may be in glottal fry (see Chapter 2). It's as if you are taking the line back. You start to give it to your partner or the audience, then change your mind, become self-conscious, run out of energy, or lose interest in the subject. A whole speech or song done in this manner is tedious at best, for both the audience and the vocal mechanism, although performers who use this pattern habitually are seldom aware of what they are doing. To diagnose your own tendencies and work on seeing the line through:

1. Record a song or spoken monologue and observe your phrasing patterns.
2. Do something physical at the end of the line (e.g., stamp your foot, clap your hands, push on a wall).

3. Practice your piece doing push-ups or any other very demanding physical activity.
4. Work with a partner for support and feedback.

Pay particular attention to consonants at the ends of the lines. Final consonants must continue in the same direction as the rest of the line—outward—so fully produce and own every sound, including the last one. The Consonants Only exercise can help you to isolate consonant sounds and to separate them from the vowels. This is especially necessary in singing. If you even think the consonant that is coming up, your articulators will move in that direction and color your vowel; if the vowel is not pure, what you are saying will not be clear and your voice will not sound its best. The vowels are your friends! Your voice sings on the vowels and each vowel must be specific, never *sort of.* When you clarify the vowels and make each consonant clean and specific, you do wonderful things for your voice and clarify the text at the same time. You might think of final consonants as hanging out in space, separated from the sounds before them.

The Legato Line

The ability to produce a legato line is basic to the singer's development of a solid vocal technique. That same skill is essential for speaking. Legato requires a real connection from one note or sound to another, without any interruption or hesitation, and without even the tiniest stopping of the voice or addition of air to emphasize a change of note. The habit of stopping the voice slightly before words and syllables that begin with a vowel—and frequently using a harsh glottal attack for the upcoming vowel—is particularly ingrained and problematic in some American speech. Awareness of that tendency and work with an excellent teacher will help you to understand the feeling of legato, and you will immediately notice your ability to phrase language so that it flows. The Vowels Only exercise is also brilliant for working on a legato line. Although we definitely emphasize words and syllables in a variety of ways, legato is the norm and should be habitual. When we accent syllables arbitrarily and unconsciously as a result of poor technique, our intended emphases lose their impact and we muddle the text.

Summary

Once the voice is working well and your speech skills are in order, you will have the flexibility and self-knowledge to work with text on a more advanced level. You will research roles and their dialects, learn languages, work on different styles of material, and probably explore a variety of approaches to voice, movement, and acting. Through it all and throughout your career, you must also maintain a professional level of fitness and aliveness as you continually refine what you understand as technical *truth*. When you perform you will not think technique, but in your private work you must stay in touch with the basic technical skills that support you as an artist. At the same time, always allow yourself a sense of wonder and the right to be *wrong*, for technically perfect performances are often dull!

Recommended Reading

Berry, C. 1973. *Voice and the Actor.* New York: Macmillan.

———. 1992. *The Actor and the Text.* New York: Applause Books.

———. 2001. *Text in Action.* London: Virgin Publishing.

Linklater, K. 1976. *Freeing the Natural Voice.* New York: Drama Books.

———. 1992. *Freeing Shakespeare's Voice.* New York: Theatre Communications Group.

Rodenburg, P. 1992. *The Right to Speak.* London: Methuen Drama.

———. 1993. *The Need for Words.* New York: Routledge.

———. 1998. *The Actor Speaks.* London: Methuen Drama.

———. 2002. *Speaking Shakespeare.* London: Methuen Drama.

7 ■ Singing and Acting

Overview

When singing is isolated from acting, an essential dimension is missing. Yet relatively few singers are actually trained as actors and many singers have misconceptions about what it means *to act*. So what is acting? Does it depend on the approach, the training, the method? Yes, and no. There are common denominators that enable us to recognize excellence across a wide range of approaches to the craft.

Perhaps the bottom line in *acting* is believability, even with very stylized material. Is the listener engaged? Does the singer communicate so that we easily suspend disbelief and take the journey of the song, aria, duet, with her or him? Or are we thinking, "There goes that gesture he makes regardless of what he sings"; "Oh, she is about to take a breath so here goes another gasp"; "He always seems so fake, so pompous"; or "She's so rigid she couldn't possibly be having an affair with anyone!"—none of which has anything to do with the music itself.

Theatre is about extraordinary events and experiences. It's about conflict and desire. It's about human, or superhuman, beings who *act* to make things happen. When we act, or take *action*, we turn our attention away from ourselves and toward other beings; we lose *self-consciousness* and become *other conscious*.

How many of us have been told by an acting or singing teacher, "Don't listen to yourself"? Of course we hear ourselves, but it is only when we go beyond the point of monitoring and editing ourselves that we begin to communicate. Indeed, it is only when we focus outside ourselves that we actually take the journey of the song and feel that wonderful connection to our partner onstage and to the audience. It is only when we lose ourselves that we begin to manifest the artist and *act*—by whatever method or approach we choose.

A Formula That Works

In his 1997 book, *True and False,* David Mamet said:

> *The actor is onstage to communicate the play to the audience. That is the beginning and the end of his and her job. To do so the actor needs a strong voice, superb diction, a supple, well-proportioned body, and a rudimentary understanding of the play (1997, 9).*

I emphatically suggest that if what we communicate as singers has little or nothing to do with the play or the poem, we are not acting. Nor are we interesting.

VOICE AND DICTION

1. "A strong voice" might be paraphrased as "sufficiently well-trained and appropriate for the part."
2. "Superb diction" in the context of communication requires a thorough understanding of the text and *word stress* that is appropriate to the language. In English, for example, singers frequently stress all the syllables and words as if they were equal, and give particular stress to whatever goes up in pitch—not because it is important, but because our voices tend to get louder on high pitches if they are not directed to do otherwise.

   An excellent way to undo this unconscious habit is to speak the piece as monologue—preferably before learning the music so that the musical rhythm is not yet habit. Also, avoid emphasizing obvious poetic rhythms, unless they are essential to the style of the piece. The monologue should be directed to a specific person, real or imagined, in a specific setting, and you must *want* something from that person! Specificity is essential— that is, know exactly who your partner is, what you want, and why you must communicate these thoughts and feelings to that person at this moment. What do you want to happen as a result of your speaking/singing these words (e.g., he won't leave me, the war will end, I'll get the part, she'll say she loves me too)? Playing generalities and moods is not believable and comes across as fake. So we do not play emotions or states of being, as in *acting* sad, happy, afraid, shy, nervous, giddy. Rather, we play *actions* so that the *audience* can experience the sadness, happiness, fear, and so on. Our job is to *communicate* the play to the audience.

One way of doing the monologue exercise is to write out the text on one side of the page and list *actions* on the other side. By actions, I mean active verbs, as in *to kick, to squeeze, to seduce, to embrace*—there are hundreds of possibilities. The verb must be something you could do *physically* to your partner. As in the case of *to kick*, you will not actually kick your partner, but words can kick—or embrace, or entertain, or frighten, or fascinate. The *actions* are tactics used to get what you want. As in real life, we do not play the same action all the time. When one thing is not working or has been used long enough, we play something else in order to keep the partner interested.

The monologue exercise can turn even a song or aria that has been done by everybody into *your* song—not by rearranging the music or doing away with traditional or musical parameters, but by finding your own relationship to the text within the prescribed style and genre. It is important to know that there is no *right* set of actions. We can play *any action* on any line! For example, take a statement found, in some form, in music of virtually every genre and style: "I love you." These words can be played to embrace, to stun, to surprise, to frighten, to entertain, to cajole, to kick, to embarrass, to seduce, to hurt, to tease, and on and on, and they will have very different meanings according to the way they are played.

One of the most powerful devices for moving you toward acting the piece is the use of *operative* words. We use operative words all the time when we speak. Operative words are the words we emphasize, and one or two per phrase is average. Too often in singing, all the words become equal, which is totally unreal. So even if you do nothing with the piece but use operative words, your performance will be transformed. Do not be concerned with the *right* operative word. What is stressed naturally will depend on your relationship to the text and your partner; therefore, your operative words may be different from those chosen by another actor.

Go through your song and underline or circle the operative words. Then speak the text and notice how the language flows, or drives toward those important words. Now sing the text using the pitches, but not necessarily the rhythms, of the song. Instead, keep your speech rhythms intact as you sing. Finally, sing the piece and use the musical rhythms, but do not let the music overpower the phrasing and *sense* you have found in your work with operative words. Even when words or syllables are sustained, if they are not strong in terms of sense, do not stress them; and if an operative word falls on a quick note, you must still give it more weight than the little connecting words around it.

THE BODY AND THE PLAY

3. "A supple, well-proportioned body" does not mean that every singer/actor needs to be gorgeous. It does mean daily, conscious work on your body. It means training in

stage movement and characterization and a lifetime of keeping fit and healthy. The body is the actor's instrument and the voice is not separate from it. In *The Actor and the Text*, Cicely Berry says:

> . . . *[W]e have to find ways to get . . . [words] not only on our tongue, but to make them part of our whole physical self in order to release them from the tyranny of the mind (1992, 22).*

So acting is not just a head thing; indeed, it is a very visceral activity.

A wonderful exercise that you can use with almost any kind of material is *physicalizing* the text. There are no strict rules about the exercise, except that there should be total freedom of movement. No plans, no choreogrphy, just allow your body to move—to play—without logic while speaking or singing. Remember your body is more than just arms and legs, and there are *levels* in space through which you can move. So you might start on the floor, sitting or lying down, or on all fours, or hang over in a drop-down. The work is exploratory, exhilarating, and fun! Use the exercise on your own or with a class. Physicalizing the text is also great with duets and other scene work and can help enormously to establish a physical relationship between partners.

Now sing the song or speak the speech in a more *normal* way but with the same physical energy informing the text, the actions, and the emotional connection to what is happening. Almost invariably you—and your voice—will be much more *alive* and interesting after the physicalization, and chances are you will have discovered some things about the piece that you never noticed before.

4. "A *rudimentary* understanding of the play" means you don't sing the aria without knowing the opera. You don't sing the song without knowing the musical. You don't

sing whatever you sing without knowing who you are, where you are, what you want, and why.

Summary

The availability of a well-trained voice, superb diction, a fit body, and an understanding of the play goes a long way toward helping the singer to *act*. In addition, *other consciousness*—focusing outside ourselves—is essential. The audience is willing to suspend disbelief. They want to take the journey. Acting is not about what *we feel* as singers; it's about what the *audience feels* when we sing.

The study of acting can be invaluable for singers. It can add an amazing dimension to your art and to your life, as can the study of singing for actors! There are many different and valid approaches to the craft of acting and the reading of any book is no substitute for working with excellent teachers. May this chapter whet your appetite for the real thing!

References

Berry, C. 1992. *The Actor and the Text.* New York: Applause Books.

Mamet, D. 1997. *True and False.* New York: Pantheon Books.

PART III

Additional Perspectives

8 ■ Special Considerations

Overcoming Fears about Singing

Singing can be scary. We make a lot of noise and tend to call attention to ourselves when we sing. Singing requires a certain confidence and many times that confidence has been effectively undermined by a careless comment at some point in our lives. We are not our voices, but it is easy to feel as if we are because voice is integral to who we are, to how we perceive ourselves, and to how we are perceived by others. In Western cultures, singing tends to be set apart and considered special and we compare our own voices to those of the singers we admire most and have heard primarily on well-engineered recordings. Singing may even be a form of voice use that we experience rarely (e.g., at birthdays and Christmas), whereas we may speak every day, unconsciously and confidently.

Some performers, of course, are actually more comfortable singing than speaking, and if you have sung a lot for audiences, you may feel much safer singing a song than doing a spoken monologue! Music can serve as a kind of mask for whatever imperfections or insecurities we perceive in ourselves; we can *lose* ourselves in the beauty and texture and even technical games of the music, whereas speaking can seem mundane, awkward, and formless in comparison. The singer who has not been trained to speak onstage may feel very exposed when speech is required, just as the actor who has not been trained to sing onstage feels extremely vulnerable when singing is required. Wherever you are on the continuum, I suggest that you sing, speak, and just enjoy making vocal sounds in your daily workout so that the sensations of singing and speaking as a performer will become more familiar and less daunting. In addition, note the following:

1. Individual work with the right teacher can make a world of difference in your level of skill and confidence as a singer.
2. Classes in theatre voice and acting open up a new world of sound and vocal possibility, regardless of your primary focus as a performer.
3. Singing in an ensemble, and learning to *hold* a part will prepare you for shows that require you to sing in a group and harmonize with the main melody.

Many actors start out as nonsingers, but in the course of their training become, not only proficient, but brilliant at using their voices to sing. Careers frequently take off in new directions and there is, invariably, the realization that singing is not at all separate from the rest of your work as an actor.

Extending Kinesthetic Awareness

Singing requires more continuous use of the mechanism than any other vocal activity and tends to involve a wider range of pitch and volume as well. Singing in a healthy manner can strengthen the rest of your vocal technique. If you are not accustomed to singing, however, you may experience some new physical sensations, and being able to distinguish between healthy and unhealthy sound production in your own body is critical to developing a good vocal technique. What we feel when we sing is essentially an extension of what we feel when we speak, but we tend to notice our sensations more during singing because of the continuous nature of that activity. Figuring out the *right* sensations for healthy vocal production is a personal and ongoing process, and involves an element of trial and error, as you respond to the demands of a career and natural changes within your body. Even so, there are a few simple guidelines that can keep you relatively safe regardless of the style of music you are singing:

1. If it hurts, don't do it! If the way you are singing hurts your throat or otherwise makes you feel *strained*, chances are there's something about what you're doing that isn't entirely efficient.

2. If you lose part of your range or your ability to speak comfortably after you've been singing for a while, that may be a warning signal.

3. Listen to your body, and know that *pushing* or continuing to sing in a way that hurts is not going to make things better and can do some serious damage over time.

4. Do not expect singing to happen on its own. Singing takes a physical commitment, and like any other athletic activity, requires energy and selective attention. We *do* something physically when we sing, speak, laugh, cry, or otherwise use our voices, and *what* we do habitually defines our vocal technique.

All of your work on alignment, range, resonance, and articulation can contribute immeasurably to your ability to distinguish *good* from *bad* sensations when you sing. Still it is easy to be confused because you are listening periodically, as well as feeling, and cannot hear yourself as others hear you (see Chapter 2). Therefore, even as a seasoned performer, you will want to have regular or occasional sessions with a valued teacher. Another pair of ears and eyes can spark your own awareness and help you to maintain a healthy approach to using your voice throughout a long career.

Singing as a Diagnostic Tool

Singing can serve as an excellent diagnostic tool for the overall soundness of a vocal technique. When we speak, we frequently get away with certain technical inefficiencies, but the minute we start to sing, those flaws become magnified. Singing can act as a mirror to the rest of the technique and thus help identify and solve technical problems that might otherwise go unnoticed. The continuous and demanding nature of singing requires an excellence and refinement of technique that might be compared to the ability to speak a lengthy and very fast text with ease and brilliance in a large space. Breath management has to be efficient, alignment is critical, a wide pitch range is necessary, and articulators must function at a high level of development and skill. Each performer's feelings about singing, however, must be factored into the diagnostic equation; therefore, acknowledgment and acceptance of those feelings is essential.

EXERCISES

The following practical exercises integrate, refine, and simplify the technical elements of vocal production as they pave the way for a discussion of techniques for extreme voice use, or *extended vocal gesture*, which is discussed in Chapter 9.

Humming Glissandos

When you have not used your voice for an hour or so during the day, do some glissandos (sirens) humming very quietly (throat open, space between your teeth) as you connect to abdominal action and efficient breath management. You can do glissandos almost anywhere (e.g., sitting in a restaurant, walking across a campus, on the way to rehearsal, in the hallway or waiting room of a casting agent). This simple exercise can reconnect you to the energy and readiness you felt at the conclusion of your warm-up earlier in the day. It can also focus your voice and integrate your range very quickly for singing or speaking.

By now, you should have developed a personal routine that fully incorporates vocal sounds and articulatory gymnastics with physical exercises for strength, flexibility, and stamina. In the course of that warm-up, you should also have begun to focus on the particular work you are doing as an actor, so as you prepare your body and voice, you also prepare yourself mentally and emotionally for the work ahead. Before doing the following exercise, be sure you have warmed up thoroughly at some point during the day.

Monitoring

This exercise is wonderful done in a class with at least three other students monitoring what is happening physically as you sing or speak; or you may do it on your own once you know the exercise. Sit on a chair, away from the chair back, with good alignment, pelvic floor lifted, and the back of your neck long and flexible. You will *be very still* throughout the exercise. Sing or speak your text with great internal energy, but no excess physical motion. One classmate should monitor your head/neck position, another your ribs, and another your abdominal action. You may want to have a fourth person at your feet noticing what is happening in the lower body as you use your voice. Monitors may touch—gently, of course—to encourage ease and efficiency in your physical effort; as you speak or sing they should be particularly aware of any tendency you may have to:

- thrust your head forward
- lift your chin
- tense and/or overuse your jaw
- furrow your brow
- pull your tongue back
- tense your shoulders and/or upper chest
- make noisy inhalations
- hold your belly tight
- tense your buttocks and/or thighs
- squeeze your toes
- make generic motions or nervous gestures

Have another class member act as your partner to help you focus outside yourself and on what you are doing as an actor. The need to communicate can streamline your technique, so *allow* your body to work as monitors observe your technical process.

Once you have done your song or spoken monologue, ask the monitors and your partner for feedback. Let them know about your experience with the exercise as well. When you are able to sit virtually motionless and just focus on interacting with your partner, suddenly you will know exactly what is necessary technically, and what is superfluous. Your body will do only what it needs to do, and that can be very revealing. You might think of this as an advanced version of simply observing the way your body breathes (see Chapter 1). The obstructions are gone. There's only breath and text and your need to communicate.

9 ■ The Whole Voice

Overview

Actor training programs frequently include techniques for every possible use of the voice except singing, and training curricula for singers seldom include theatre voice. Acting for Singers is becoming a regularly required course for many opera majors but is seldom supported by the prerequisites of theatre voice and movement. Likewise, singing is often available as a peripheral and/or optional course in actor training but is seldom supported by appropriate connecting links to the rest of the actor's work. Singing and speaking are accomplished by the same instrument; we can move easily from one activity to the other in the same breath; and singing and speaking onstage have similar technical requirements. Therefore, learning these and other vocal activities from a similar perspective can increase your overall level of skill, flexibility, and confidence, both onstage and off.

One Technical Core

The voice is the body, in that (1) vocal production is a physical activity, and (2) physical position and movement can directly affect the sound of the voice.

We use our bodies in an infinite variety of ways and vocal technique can be approached effectively from more than one direction. For the performer whose career requires a certain versatility, however, a technical core that is both flexible and secure can be an invaluable asset. Breath use is at the heart of vocal technique and knowing how to handle each performance situation, consciously or unconsciously, in terms of breath use, usually requires training, experience, and a willingness to be simple. The body itself is the ultimate teacher; wise practitioners can act as critical guides and we must be our own coaches every day as we work to meet the demands and achieve the goals of our respective careers.

Singing and speaking are by no means the only vocal sounds we make, but they form a nucleus and require a technique that can act as a central core from which we deviate consciously for other vocal activities. Maintaining the same basic technique for singing and speaking, and integrating that technique with requirements for dance and movement, is essential for the musical theatre actor. Working from one technical core can also be infinitely freeing for both the classical singer and the actor whose focus is not musical theatre.

Expanding the Vocal Parameters

Singing and speaking tend to occur over long periods of time in the context of performance, while other vocal activities are usually shorter in duration. Some vocal sounds do not have labels and require no special attention; others, such as laughing, crying, shouting, and screaming, are more specific and fall into the category of *extended* voice use. Techniques for extended voice use are best learned one on one with an experienced practitioner; however, certain principles regarding the production of extended sounds are worth noting and the following observations may serve as a valuable reference.

LAUGHING AND CRYING

Laughing and crying[1] both occur on the end of the breath rather than on a full or deep breath. If you breathe as if you were going to

[1] This section is drawn primarily from the Fitzmaurice approach. Catherine Fitzmaurice, "Breathing is Meaning," *The Vocal Vision*, ed. by Marion Hampton and Barbara Acker. (New York: Applause, 1997, pp. 247–252).

sing or speak a long phrase then start to laugh or cry, you will probably sound very fake! Your facial expressions, like the masks of comedy and tragedy, are also essential elements in the physicality of these actions. Both laughing and crying start in the belly, but somewhat higher in the belly than singing and speaking; the abdominal action for laughing and crying is more in the area of a pant. There are many kinds of laughs, of course, and crying in different contexts requires different kinds of noises. Still, the general principle of working on little to no air and starting the laugh or cry in the upper belly with quick, tremorlike activity (but not an actual tremor) will take you wherever you need to go almost instantly. So your breathing for laughing and crying is shallow and your inhalations may be noisy gasps! Obviously, text done within a laugh or cry may be broken up into short phrases because you are not fueling the voice with enough breath to sustain phrases of much length. However, if you are speaking in a large space, you will probably use a combination of abdominal actions in order to be heard and understood within the laugh or cry.

The throat position for laughing and crying is quite open; indeed laughing and/or crying slightly throughout a song, as an exercise, can help you to find space, or openness, in the area of the pharynx and soft palate. *Focus* in the voice is critical for clarity of speech within a laugh or cry. In addition, your articulation must be extremely efficient because you are distorting the usual sound of your voice and need to communicate through that distortion.

SHOUTING AND SCREAMING

The untrained actor—or football fan—often becomes hoarse after shouting. Even actors who are developing a solid technical foundation otherwise, often will shout with considerable tension in strategic parts of the body and with insufficient air to support the volume and overall power required for shouting. Shouting or screaming onstage, poorly done, hurts both the actor and the audience because we physically feel the way another person produces sound. As an aside, it is this phenomenon that allows us to understand immediately what our students are doing and, in reverse, to copy the sounds of other actors and singers, including our teachers.

Making loud noises on stage safely and effectively requires a deepening of the basic technique you have already acquired. For shouting and screaming, your breath must be deep and efficiently managed, your body cannot get away with any unnecessary tension, your throat must be wide open, and your tongue must remain forward rather than pulling back into your mouth. Focus, or forward *placement*, of the sound is essential for maximum brilliance with minimum effort, and brilliance is what you need in order to be both heard and understood at an extreme level of loudness. As with laughing and crying, your speech energy must be superb. A particular note of caution is in order regarding the position of your head and neck. Even the slightest tendency to shorten the back of your neck and press the head forward can undo all the rest of your technique. Be sure you are able to do the Monitoring exercise at the end of Chapter 8 *easily* before attempting to shout or scream.

Shouting does not need to be high in pitch and is usually far more powerful and effective when it is not. So you will need to work on separating the elements of pitch, pace, and volume in order to combine them appropriately for what you are doing. Specific exercises in the independent use and combining of pitch, pace, and volume are beyond the scope of this book; they can be learned in individual coaching sessions and in workshops focusing on advanced vocal techniques for actors and singers.

Screaming, on the other hand, is usually done in a very high pitch range and is often considered the most extreme and demanding of vocal gestures. As with laughing and crying, the context of the scream will influence its character, but a *classic* scream has a high, clear core, plus enough noise, or turbulence, to make it convincing. The core sound is very similar to a high note that is sung (without vibrato), and men can scream in either their falsetto or modal (regular) quality. Rounded positions are particularly useful for finding easy high pitches, and puppy yelps take some people right to the center of the scream. As with shouting, your body must be free of unnecessary tension, your ribs and abdomen must be functioning at peak efficiency, and your throat must be open and available to act as a channel for this totally involving sound. The following are key points to remember:

1. Work on screaming with a highly experienced teacher.
2. *Never* scream unless you are fully warmed up!
3. When you scream, go for it! Don't stand back and watch yourself. Your whole being must be committed to what you are doing.
4. Drink plenty of water as soon as possible after screaming; your throat may feel a bit scratchy from the noise element of this sound.
5. Do not scream, or practice screaming, for long periods of time.
6. Use humming glissandos or other simple, quiet vocalises to cool down after screaming, and check to be sure that you can still sing and speak your lowest notes.

Shouting and screaming are particularly energizing activities and the total commitment required for their execution can take you to a new level of awareness and confidence.

Sounds of combat, or fight noises, are also a regular part of theatre voice training and require similar techniques to shouting and screaming. A variety of different techniques may be needed for such unusual sounds as keening and kulning, but with a solid foundation and excellent physical skills, you should be able to explore these and other extended vocal activities with relative ease and safety.

■ ■ ■

Summary

Discovering and using everything our voices can do is probably an impossible, though fascinating, ideal. Expanding the voice training of actors to include singing techniques and incorporating theatre voice into the curricula of singers, however, is neither impossible nor idealistic. Indeed, it is infinitely practical from the performer's point of view, and the time is right for us to move in that direction.

Communication among voice professionals is being actively encouraged at national and international conferences and acknowledgment of the physical, movement-related aspects of vocal production is reflected in many training programs throughout the world. Accessing and using the whole voice, however, is ultimately an individual matter, in that it may involve experiencing voice in a new way. As a final exercise: (1) Take a single phrase of text and alternate speaking and singing it on the *same breath* and with the *same technique*. (2) Extend that process to several lines of text and allow your body to move freely in an undirected manner as you sing and speak. (3) Continue the exercise entirely in your less comfortable mode (singing or speaking). (4) Explore the text through any sounds you like as you enjoy the total involvement of sounding and moving!

Suggested Reading

Melton, J. 2001. "Sing Better, Work More." *Voice and Speech Review*. New York: Applause Books.

■ Appendix

Organizations That Focus on Care
of the Professional Voice

The Australian Voice Association (AVA), General Secretariat,
2nd floor, 11–19 Bank Place, Melbourne VIC 3000, Australia;
www.australianvoiceassociation.com.au.

The British Voice Association (BVA), 330 Gray's Inn Road,
London WC1X 8EE, England;
www.british-voice-association.com.

Canadian Voice Care Foundation (CVCF), 2828 Toronto
Crescent NW, Calgary, AB T2N 3W2, Canada;
www.canadianvoicecarefdn.com.

The Voice Foundation, 1721 Pine Street, Philadelphia, PA 19103,
USA; *www.voicefoundation.org.*